The rise and fall of languages

This book offers a new approach to language change, the punctuated equilibrium model. This is based on the premise that during most of the 100,000 or more years that humans have had language, states of equilibrium have existed during which linguistic features diffused across the languages in a given area so that they gradually converged on a common prototype. From time to time, the state of equilibrium would be punctuated, with expansion and split of peoples and of languages. Most recently, as a result of European colonisation and the globalisation of communication, many languages currently spoken face imminent extinction. Professor Dixon suggests that every linguist should assume a responsibility for documenting some of these languages before they disappear.

Professor Dixon argues that the commonly used family tree model of language change is appropriate during a period of punctuation, but not during the longer periods of equilibrium. He suggests that many of the views currently held by linguists, archaeologists and geneticists need serious rethinking, and emphatically dismisses recent speculation that the original languages of humankind could be reconstructed.

The rise and fall of languages

R. M. W. DIXON

Australian National University

CAMBRIDGE
UNIVERSITY PRESS

PUBLISHED BY THE PRESS SYNDICATE OF THE UNIVERSITY OF CAMBRIDGE
The Pitt Building, Trumpington Street, Cambridge CB2 IRP, United Kingdom

CAMBRIDGE UNIVERSITY PRESS
The Edinburgh Building, Cambridge CB2 2RU, United Kingdom
40 West 20th Street, New York, NY 10011–4211, USA
10 Stamford Road, Oakleigh, Melbourne 3166, Australia

First published 1997
Reprinted 1999

Printed in the United Kingdom at the University Press, Cambridge

Typeset in Concorde BQ, 8.5/13pt, in QuarkXpress™   [SE]

A catalogue record for this book is available from the British Library

Library of Congress cataloguing in publication data

Dixon, Robert M. W.
The rise and fall of languages / R. M. W. Dixon.
   p.   cm.
Includes bibliographical references (p. 153) and index.
ISBN 0 521 62310 3 (hardback). – ISBN 0 521 62654 4 (paperback)
1. Historical linguistics.   2. Comparative linguistics.
I. Title.
P140.D59   1997
417′.7–dc21   97–23092   CIP

ISBN 0 521 62310 3 hardback
ISBN 0 521 62654 4 paperback

Contents

Acknowledgements vi

1 **Introduction** *1*

2 **Preliminaries** *7*

3 **Linguistic areas and diffusion** *15*
   3.1 What can diffuse *19*
   3.2 Languages in contact *22*

4 **The family tree model** *28*
   4.1 Criteria *30*
   4.2 Proto-languages *45*
   4.3 Dating *46*
   4.4 Subgrouping *49*

5 **Modes of change** *54*
   5.1 Changes within languages *54*
   5.2 Language splitting *58*
   5.3 The origin of language *63*

6 **The punctuated equilibrium model** *67*
   6.1 Linguistic equilibrium *68*
   6.2 Punctuation *73*
   6.3 Some examples *85*

7 **More on proto-languages** *97*

8 **Recent history** *103*

9 **Today's priorities** *116*
   9.1 Why bother? *116*
   9.2 Some modern myths *128*
   9.3 What every linguist should do *135*

10 **Summary and prospects** *139*
   10.1 The punctuated equilibrium model *139*
   10.2 Concerning comparative linguistics *140*
   10.3 Concerning descriptive linguistics *143*
   10.4 Concerning languages *145*

Appendix – where the comparative method discovery procedure fails *149*

References 153
Index 163

Acknowledgements

Alexandra Aikhenvald suggested that I should write this essay and discussed it with me at every stage, supplying ideas, many examples, and tempered criticism. She has provided inspiration and ongoing encouragement.

It was from talking to Peter Bellwood that I first got the idea that a model of punctuated equilibrium would help explain problems in historical linguistics that had long been a worry; he has also given valuable feedback.

The following colleagues discussed this topic with me, answered critical questions, or offered comments on a draft of the essay: Cynthia Allen, Mengistu Amberber, John Chappell, Tony Diller, Colin Groves, Deborah Hill, Hans Kuhn, Rhys Jones, Johanna Nichols, Phil Rose and Karl Rensch.

I owe a special debt to Alan Dench, Martin Duwell, Jennifer Elliott, Harold Koch, April McMahon, Jim Matisoff, Masayuki Onishi, Andrew Pawley, Calvert Watkins, and especially Lyle Campbell and Randy LaPolla – for offering detailed comments on a draft, which enabled me to add more examples and references, and to correct a number of errors.

⬤ Introduction

Current work on the relationship between languages tends to be in terms either of a family tree model of 'parent-and-child' linkage, or of a linguistic area model of the diffusion of categories and forms between adjacent languages. Family tree and linguistic area are most often treated as distinct phenomena; in this essay I will attempt to integrate them within a global view of linguistic development.

A language does not exist in a vacuum but is the means for communication within a group of people, with a certain political and economic system. An integrated theory of language development must pay attention to the way of life of the group speaking a known language, or the postulated earlier stage of a language, and their political, social and linguistic relationships with neighbouring groups speaking other languages.

The family tree model was developed for – and is eminently appropriate to – the Indo-European (IE) language family. It has become the received view of how languages are related, so that linguists attempt to discover an IE-like family tree structure in every group of languages, from anywhere in the world (whatever their typological profile); along with this goes an attempt at detailed sub-grouping. But in many cases there is no serious attempt to reconstruct part of the system of a proto-language (which is needed, as proof of a family-tree-type genetic relationship). For some groups of languages – for instance, Semitic and Polynesian – the family tree model is entirely applicable. For others it may be less so; the similarities that have been taken as evidence for genetic relationship may really be due to areal diffusion.

Approximate dates have been assigned for proto-languages –
about 6,000 years before the present (BP) for proto-Indo-European,
about 6,000 years for proto-Uralic, about 3,000 years for proto-
Algonquian, and so on. No date earlier than around 10,000 BP is
generally accepted. Yet archaeologists and human biologists believe
that humankind developed language at least 100,000 years ago (many
would put it considerably further in the past). What happened
between 100,000 years ago – or whenever language developed – and
the proto-languages of modern families, 6,000 or 10,000 years ago?
This question, which is seldom addressed in the literature, will be a
central item in the discussion below.

The parts of a proto-language that are reconstructed tend to
show tidy and homogeneous patterns, with few (if any) irregularities.
Attested spoken languages are seldom like this – there are often one
or more substrata (features from an earlier language which the given
language has replaced) or superstrata (features from another language formerly spoken within the same society by a dominant
group), and many untidy structural corners. I shall suggest that a
more realistic model of a proto-language should be developed,
paying attention to the sort of linguistic situation that may have given
rise to the proto-language, as well as what developed from it; the
former is likely to supply added insight to the latter.

How do languages change within themselves – is it a slow and
gradual process (like a slope), or do changes happen relatively suddenly, with periods of quiescence in between (like a series of steps)? I
shall suggest that although some kinds of change may be gradual –
lexical borrowing, or shift of allophones – the majority of changes
that a language undergoes are completed in a relatively short time.
These would include shift from a dependent-marking to a head-
marking profile (the development of bound pronominal elements on
the verb, and consequential dropping of case markers), shift from an
accusative to an ergative system (or vice versa), and the development
of noun classes (or genders), amongst other changes.

There is also the question of how one language becomes two,

how mutually intelligible dialects become mutually unintelligible languages. Again I suggest that this tends to happen rather rapidly, over the space of just a few generations, rather than being dragged out over centuries (with a long intermediate period when it is hard to tell whether we have one language or two).

In this book I put forward a hypothesis. Inspired by the punctuated equilibrium model in biology (first aired by Eldredge and Gould, 1972), a punctuated equilibrium model is suggested for the development (and origin) of language.[1] Over most of human history there has been an equilibrium situation. In a given geographical area[2] there would have been a number of political groups, of similar size and organisation, with no one group having undue prestige over the others. Each would have spoken its own language or dialect. They would have constituted a long-term linguistic area, with the languages existing in a state of relative equilibrium. Nothing is ever static – there would be ebbs and flows, changes and shiftings around, but in a relatively minor way. Then the equilibrium would be punctuated, and drastic changes would occur. The punctuation may be due to natural causes such as drought or flooding; or to the invention of a new tool or weapon; or to the development of agriculture; or of boats, with movement into new territories; or to the development of secular or religious imperialism. These punctuations to the state of equilibrium are likely to trigger dramatic changes within languages

[1] Here the punctuated equilibrium model is applied to the evolution and split of languages. It can also be applied at other levels, although this is not discussed here. For instance, Goodenough (1992) describes how a quiescent period within a language may involve small phonetic changes that will cumulate in a sudden and radical phonological restructuring, also leading to radical morphological and lexical restructuring.

[2] A geographical area in which linguistic equilibrium is established will be a region within which there is relatively easy communication – typically an island, or a river basin, or else an area enclosed by barriers to communication such as the sea on one side and a mountain range on another side. Such an area will generally be fairly homogeneous in terms of terrain, climate and food resources, e.g. a region of jungle may comprise one linguistic area, an adjacent region of grasslands another area, and a mountainous tableland region another area.

and between languages. They give rise to expansion and split of peoples and of languages. It is during a period of punctuation – which will be brief in comparison with the eras of equilibrium that precede and follow – that the family tree model applies.

I suggest that, during a period of equilibrium, linguistic features tend to diffuse across the languages of a given area so that – over a very long period – they converge on a common prototype. Then, during a period of punctuation – characterised by expansion and split – a series of new languages will develop, diverging from a common proto-language.

This hypothesis naturally extends to the question of the origin of language. There are competing possibilities. One is that language developed to its modern form very gradually – adding a few hundred words and a few new bits of grammar every few millennia – going from rudimentary to primitive to post-primitive to pre-modern to modern. I opt for the alternative scenario. Early humans lived in a state of relative equilibrium, with developing cognitive and communicative ability but no language. Then, by some process of punctuation, language developed. I suggest that it would have developed rather fast, and that within a few centuries (maybe within a few generations) there would have been something recognisable not as some kind of primitive speech but as a fairly fully developed language, comparable in degree of complexity with languages spoken today. There would then have ensued another period of equilibrium.

A likely response to the idea of a punctuated equilibrium model of language development goes as follows. If the history of human languages, over 100,000 or more years, has been characterised by long periods of equilibrium, how is it that we see nothing of this around us today? The answer is straightforward. The last 2,000 years – and especially the last few hundred – have been the scene of a spectacular punctuation (such as is unlikely ever to have occurred before). The rise of world religions, imperialism, guns, writing, and other factors, have combined in such a way that some people and their languages have grown more powerful, and swept all else before them. We – as a people who write and read and study linguistics – are an integral part of this phenomenon. When Europeans intrude into some new part of the world they provide a violent punctuation. By the time scientific observers arrive (or even by the fact of their arrival), the social and linguistic equilibrium is destroyed. But it can, with careful attention, be reconstructed. A major factor in turning me towards a punctuated equilibrium hypothesis of language development has been the experience of trying (over a period of 30 years) to make sense of the linguistic situation in Aboriginal Australia, a continent whose people had only minimal contact with the rest of the world for tens of millennia. We can see here, in retrospect, a prototypical linguistic diffusion area that was in a state of equilibrium. The same may have been true of the linguistic situation in other parts of the world; these will only be recognisable if viewed in an appropriate way.

The implications of a punctuated equilibrium model of language development are as follows. Family tree models, with a number of daughter languages diverging from a common proto-language, are only appropriate for periods of punctuation. In the intervening periods of equilibrium, linguistic areas are built up by the diffusion of features, and the languages in a given area will gradually converge towards a common prototype. Thus, the family tree model has a limited applicability in the context of the overall development of human languages over the past 100,000 or more years. The limits of reconstruction are, in fact, modest. Unfortunately, there has been a tendency to see family trees as the only model of language development; the model has been overapplied, producing 'results' that are not scientifically valid.

The final part of this essay looks at the linguistic picture today, where in every continent languages are dead, dying or endangered. It asks what it will take for a language to survive. The answer is grim (but it should be faced). There is then discussion of the major priority that should confront people who call themselves linguists. This is to get out into the field, and to provide description of some part of the wealth of human language, documenting the diversity before it is – as it will be – lost. Finally, I draw together conclusions about what work is needed if we are to achieve a better understanding of the development of language, in general and in particular instances.

A warning is in order at this point. Many of the things I say and the conclusions that are drawn will be regarded as 'politically unacceptable' in the context of today's world. In addition, many groups of linguists may be offended by what is said about their area of specialisation. This is, unfortunately, an inevitable consequence of trying to look at the question of language development in global perspective, of attempting an honest appraisal of the present state of comparative – and other branches of – linguistics, and of giving a projection of the future fates of languages.

② Preliminaries

The word 'language' is used in at least two rather different senses. There is the political sense where each nation or tribe likes to say that it speaks a different language from its neighbours. And there is the linguistic sense where two forms of speech which are mutually intelligible are regarded as dialects of a single language. Typically, several 'languages' in the political sense may each be a dialect of one language in the linguistic sense. For instance, in Australia there were about 700 tribal nations but only, in total, around 260 languages (in the linguistic sense). They were typically a number of adjacent communities speaking mutually intelligible dialects of a single language. Swedish and Norwegian are separate political 'languages' but could be regarded as dialects of one linguistic language. The opposite situation is found more rarely – because China is one nation, people sometimes talk of Mandarin, Cantonese, Min, Wu, etc., as dialects of a single 'language', in the political sense; they are, in fact, not mutually intelligible and are separate languages, by the linguistic definition.

In the remainder of this book the term 'language' is used in its linguistic sense; two forms of speech which are mutually intelligible are regarded as dialects of one language. Once political considerations are firmly discarded, it is generally not a difficult matter to decide whether one is dealing with one language or with more than one in a given situation. A speaker of one variety can be given a spoken or written passage in another variety, and their comprehension tested by a series of questions. Certain allowances have to be made, especially for habits of pronunciation. A speaker of English from New Orleans might, at first, experience some difficulty in understanding the English spoken in Glasgow (and vice versa); but, after a few days of phonetic acclimatisation, comprehension should be at the 80–90% level.

There can be other complications, of course. One involves dialect chains, where speakers of X and Y can understand each other, and so do speakers of Y and Z, but dialects X and Z are scarcely mutually intelligible. And, rather rarely, intelligibility may be higher in one direction. For instance, speakers of Portuguese can understand Spanish but this applies less well the other way around. (Part of the reason is that Spanish has – in certain respects – a more conservative structure; it effectively retains the underlying forms, to which Portuguese has applied various diachronic changes. Compare Spanish *mano* 'hand' and *color* 'colour' with Portuguese *mão* and *cor.* It is easier to understand another variety when one has to apply certain rules of change – Spanish to Portuguese – than when one has to unravel changes – Portuguese to Spanish.) Each of these situations – dialect chains and one-way intelligibility – constitutes a marginal situation. A decision (which may be fairly arbitrary) has to be taken, and consistently applied, about whether to talk of one language or more than one in such cases; I opt for the 'one language' decision.

I said that, leaving aside these difficult cases (which are rather rare), there is generally little difficulty in deciding on what is a language. This is because communication is typically a fairly cut-and-dried matter. The reader may have experienced what it is like to learn a language after childhood. At first one understands almost nothing of what is said around one, or what one reads; then, quite suddenly, one understands a great deal of what one hears (if it is not spoken too fast) or reads. It is the same between users of two speech varieties: they either understand very little (maybe 10%) – here we have different languages – or almost everything (70% or more) – we are here dealing with dialects of one language. Only rather seldom does one encounter a case of around 50% intelligibility. This is consistent with the suggestion that, when one language splits into two, this happens rather rapidly, over just a few generations, rather than being a long-drawn-out process.

I shall make the following basic assumptions, which underlie what follows.

Assumption 1

Every language, and every dialect within a language, is always in a state of change. The speech of each generation is slightly different from that of the preceding one.

Assumption 2

The rate at which a language changes is not constant and is not predictable.[1] Rather, it depends on many factors, especially upon what other language(s) speakers of the given language are in contact with. Generally, a language with no immediate neighbours is likely to change relatively slowly (e.g. Icelandic, where the existence of a well-developed literary tradition has also played a major role in dampening change); and, if there are neighbours, the rate of change is likely to relate to how different in structure these other languages are, and to how much bilingualism there is.[2] Another factor is the speakers' attitude towards their own language and towards other languages; and, as a related factor, the 'language policy' of the government. A non-prestige language (or dialect) is likely to change to become more similar to a prestige language (or dialect) which is known to most of its speakers. (The reverse situation is unlikely to

[1] Note also that different parts of a language may change at different rates. In one language, verbs may change more rapidly than nouns, while this may be reversed in another language.

[2] For instance, English has long been the prestige language in Hong Kong, and most people try to learn it, but there seems to have been very little English influence (other than loan words) on Cantonese. In contrast, in Taiwan, where Mandarin is the prestige language and Taiwanese was actively suppressed for more than forty years, each of the two languages has been heavily influenced by the other, so that they have become more alike. (Randy LaPolla, personal communication.)

occur simply because speakers of a prestige language seldom need to, and almost never care to, learn a non-prestige language that is spoken nearby – see §6.2.)

An unusual example of rapid change concerns Muyuw, an Austronesian language spoken on Woodlark Island, off the coast of New Guinea. Lithgow (1973) reports that about 13% of the vocabulary was replaced over a period of 50 years or less. There have also been significant grammatical changes – for instance, the old way of saying 'my knee' was *gun-kitut* (lit. 'my-knee') whereas the new way is *kitʌtu-gw* (lit. 'knee-my'). The changes were so great that a man who returned to the island after an absence of 15 years could not at first be fully understood. Lithgow comments that 'speakers love to borrow from adjacent languages and dialects, either from boredom, from social pressure, or from a desire to display their knowledge. I have heard village orators sprinkling their speeches with words from Dobu and Kilivila languages in the way that some English speakers sprinkle their discourse with snatches of French and Latin.' In this situation, social attitude engendered an accelerated rate of lexical and grammatical change.

Assumption 3

There is no universal principle that core vocabulary (the most frequently occurring lexemes – see (b) in §4.1) is less likely to be borrowed than non-core items. This does appear to hold for the languages of Europe (see Swadesh 1951) and of many other parts of the world. But it does not apply everywhere, and cannot be taken as an axiom, a partial basis for the postulation of genetic relatedness. In Australia, for instance, similar percentages of shared vocabulary are obtained by comparing 100 or 200 or 400 or 2,000 lexemes, from adjacent languages.[3]

---

[3] I have compared vocabulary between many pairs of Australian languages and obtained similar cognate percentages (to within 5%) for shorter and longer lists. Breen (1990: 54) confirms this (and see note 4 to Chapter 3 below). Comrie (1989) discusses unusual vocabulary percentages in Papuan languages, which relate to this question.

Although it scarcely needs to be said at this point in time, Assumptions 2 and 3 imply that we should pay little heed to any putative genetic links said to be justified by lexicostatistical counting, or to the putative dating of past stages of a language by the glottochronological method (see Hymes 1964: 612ff., and Bergslund and Vogt 1962). As Birnbaum (1977: 17) put it: 'the underlying supposition of a stable (or at any rate predictable) rate of linguistic change susceptible to statistical interpretation as far as the loss (and, conversely, retention) of morphemes and whole lexical items is concerned must be considered essentially false as it is controverted by factual evidence'. This is discussed further in (b) of §4.1.

I shall also follow an assumption that has generally been made in historical linguistics, but one that has been questioned recently. It is crucial for the ideas put forward in the remainder of this essay.

Assumption 4

In the normal course of linguistic evolution, each language has a single parent. That is, when two groups of people – each speaking a distinct language – merge to form one community, with a single language, this will be a genetic descendant of just one of the original languages, not of both of them equally (it is, however, likely to have a sizeable substratum or superstratum from the second language).

Thomason and Kaufman (1988), while upholding Assumption 4 in most instances of language emergence, purport to give a number of counter-examples, where a language appears to have taken its grammar and lexicon almost equally from two source languages.

One of their counter-examples is Ma'a, from Tanzania. Thomason and Kaufman characterise this as a Cushitic language that underwent massive borrowing from a Bantu language. They argue that the original language must have been Cushitic since a substantial part of the core vocabulary is Cushitic, but since the grammar is predominantly Bantu we have here a language with, effectively, two parents. Mous (1994), who has done fieldwork in this area, explains the situation in different terms. There are two registers of the Mbugu

language – a normal variety which is fully Bantu, and an 'inner'
variety (called Ma'a) which retains Bantu grammar but has a significant part of its lexicon borrowed from neighbouring Cushitic
languages. Every member of the tribe knows the normal register,
which is the unmarked variety both within the community and for
communication with neighbours who speak other Bantu languages.
Inner Mbugu (Ma'a) is known to most (not all) Mbugu and is used as
an in-group code, to distinguish the Mbugu from their Bantu-speak-
ing neighbours. Mous suggests that Inner Mbugu (Ma'a) is a special
lexical register created by speakers of Normal Mbugu, consciously
and on purpose, to set themselves apart from their neighbours. (Note
that Thomason and Kaufman's conclusion resulted partly from an
error of argumentation. Although elsewhere in their book they
mention the possibility of borrowing core vocabulary, in this instance
they appear to operate with the assumption that, since the core
vocabulary is basically Cushitic, so must the language be.[4])

Another example quoted by Thomason and Kaufman is Copper
Island Aleut, from the Bering Strait. Here the noun morphology (and
most other parts of the grammar) is from Aleut but the finite verb
morphology is from Russian, with vocabulary also coming from both
sources. This does at first sight appear to be a mixed language, with
two parents. However, Golovko (1994) sheds light on its genesis. He
explains how, on the Aleut Islands in the nineteenth century, there
were Aleut people, and Russian seal hunters/fur traders, and also a
third group, the 'creoles', who were children of Russian men and
Aleut women. The Russian-American Company (the commercial
power in the area) recognised the creoles as a special social group,
with its own privileges. Golovko relates how the creoles wanted a
distinctive ethnic identity, and suggests that for this reason they

---

[4] Kaufman (e.g. 1990: 26ff.) is a voice from the past in still maintaining a belief in
the validity of lexicostatistics and glottochronology. It is true that in some cases
these methods do give results that are compatible with those obtained from other
sources; in other cases there is wide divergence. As a consequence, they cannot
be trusted.

'invented' their own language, which may have begun as a game of code-switching and then became institutionalised. We noted earlier that every separate political group wants to have its own distinctive way of speaking (and to call this a language, using the term in the political sense). In extreme cases they may 'invent' a language to this end (here cobbling together parts from two existing languages that they know).

Assumption 4, that each language has a single parent, includes the qualification 'in the normal course of linguistic evolution'. This is intended to refer to spontaneous evolution. We do find exceptions or quasi-exceptions – like Copper Island Aleut and Inner Mbugu (Ma'a) – in cases where people purposely invent a 'mixed language', or a special language register, as a way of asserting their political identity.[5] It is likely that all the exceptions to the 'one parent' principle are of this type, being due to conscious and deliberate language engineering.[6]

A couple more preliminary points need to be made. The first is that a language can change for one of two reasons (or for a mixture of these):

(a) CONTACT-INDUCED CHANGE If some of the speakers of a given language also have some degree of competence in a second language, this may lead to lexical borrowing, allophonic shift, and also to change in grammatical categories and construction types, and some borrowing of grammatical forms. This will be discussed in the next chapter.

(b) CHANGES DUE TO THE INTERNAL DYNAMICS OF THE LANGUAGE As Baudouin de Courtenay said (Stankiewicz 1972: 63):

---

[5] There are other examples of a special language or speech style simply being invented, e.g. the Damin initiation language of the Lardil people from Australia (Hale 1973; see also Dixon 1980: 66–7), and the Tjiliwiri style of the Warlpiri people (Hale 1971). See also the papers in Bakker and Mous 1994.

[6] Creole languages often result from engineered mixing of peoples; they may constitute a further exception to 'normal course of linguistic evolution'.

'the mechanism of language (its structure and composition) at any given time is the result of all its preceding history and development, and each synchronic state determines in turn its future development'. This is clearly seen when two or more languages that are genetically related – but which have not been in contact for some time – each changes in the same way (see the classic discussion in Sapir 1921: 127–91). The phenomenon is not at present fully understood, but it seems that the languages share some common inner dynamic that engenders a certain sort of change. Examples include: (i) Grassmann's Law, deaspirating the first of two aspirated consonants in a word, applied independently in Sanskrit and Greek; (ii) the dropping of the first syllable from each word, which took place independently in separate geographical areas of Australia (Dixon 1980: 195ff.); (iii) the development of a second person singular verbal ending -*st*, independently in German and English (Greenberg 1957: 46); (iv) the same types of grammaticalisation having taken place, independently, in a number of Tibeto-Burman languages, e.g. a verb 'send' or 'give' becoming a causative marker, verbs of motion becoming directional markers on main verbs, and the development of bound pronouns (LaPolla 1994, and Matisoff 1991).

Finally, it is appropriate to make an anti-assumption, that is, to question an assumption that is frequently made (if only implicitly). This is that all language development, and all types of proof of genetic relationship, must be like what happened in the Indo-European family. As Benveniste (1966: 103) explained: 'il n'est pas certain que le modèle construit pour l'indo-européen soit le type constant de la classification génétique'. The family tree model, which so clearly explains most of the development of – and the relationships between – languages of the Indo-European family, is an important one, which has a measure of applicability in every language situation. But it is not the whole story, as the remainder of this essay will attempt to show.

③ Linguistic areas and diffusion

If two languages are in contact – some of the speakers of each having a degree of competence in the other – they are likely to borrow lexemes, grammatical categories and techniques, and some grammatical forms (in at least one direction, often in both directions) and gradually become more similar.

If a number of languages are spoken in a geographically continuous area – which contains no physical or social impediments to cross-cultural communication – there will in each language community be a degree of multilingualism. A number of linguistic traits will diffuse from language to language until each applies across a considerable region within the geographical area, sometimes across the whole area. Each language has two possible kinds of similarities to other languages[1] – genetic similarities, which are shared inheritances from a common proto-language; and areal similarities, which are due to borrowing from geographical neighbours. Emeneau (1956: 16) defined 'linguistic area' as 'an area which includes languages belonging to more than one family but showing traits in common which are found not to belong to other members of (at least) one of the families'. This is a readily recognisable area. We could equally well have an area which includes all the languages of each of several families (no language from any of the families being located outside

---

[1] There are also, of course, accidental similarities, e.g. in Mbabaram, an Australian language, the word for 'dog' is *dog* (it can be shown to have developed from an original form **gudaga* by regular phonological changes – Dixon 1991c: 362). There are also universal tendencies, such as the word for 'blow', which typically mimics the act of blowing, and often has a form something like p^hu-.

the area). If the languages from each family were scattered over the area, rather than each being in a solid block, then it might be possible to distinguish genetic from areal similarities.[2] (Lowland Amazonia is a linguistic area essentially of this type.)

It is important to note that in a linguistic area we would not expect each diffused feature to have spread into every language. Rather, each feature would have its own distribution, over most of the languages within a certain region within the area; it is the super-imposition of these individual distinctions that establishes the area as a whole.

There can also be gradation of features. Hashimoto (1976b: 50) shows how a system of tones helps to characterise China as a politically and geographically defined linguistic area. But the number of tones varies, from three in Chinese languages in the north of the area (next to languages of the Altaic type, which have no tones) to eight or nine in the south (close to languages of the Tai-Kadai family, which themselves show a multiplicity of tones).[3]

Every geographical area in which more than one language is spoken will become a linguistic area, to a greater or lesser extent. We also get areas within areas, e.g. the Balkans within Europe. Only some of these areas have been discussed in the literature. One of the best known is the north-west coast of North America, from Alaska down to northern California (e.g. Haas 1969, Sherzer 1976). Meso-America as a linguistic area is described by Campbell, Kaufman and Smith-Stark (1986).

Emeneau (1956, 1980) and Masica (1976) have delineated India

---

[2] Note though that it is frequently impossible to tell whether a point of similarity between adjacent languages is due to shared genetic retention, or to borrowing (in either direction).

[3] Tones are one of the features most open to diffusion (and thus one of the poorest indications of genetic relationship). Randy LaPolla (personal communication) reports that Qiang has tone in its southern dialects, spoken next to Chinese (and those with the most contact with Chinese have the largest number of tones and the most stable tone systems), but tones are lacking in the northern dialects.

as a linguistic area. The features here include retroflex consonants, two varieties of causative, dative subject and classifiers (the latter probably a flow-over from the south-east/east Asia linguistic area).

The Amazon basin is a rich and little-studied linguistic area. Features which are found in many languages (sometimes in just a region within this area, sometimes across the whole area) include: close central vowel, *i*; a single liquid; nasalised vowels; predominantly Consonant Vowel (CV) syllable structure; tendency to have affricates rather than fricatives; a polysynthetic verb structure with many suffixes, indicating types of modality plus location, direction, duration, iteration, etc.; subordinate clauses being shown through nominalisation, with marking on the verb; a single core argument being cross-referenced on the verb, with complex conditioning as to which argument this is, leading to ergativity splits; a distinction between alienable and inalienable possession; possessor marked on the noun by pronominal affixes identical to one of the sets marking a core argument on the verb; complex systems of classifiers and/or genders; and evidentiality (see §9.1).

In Sub-Saharan Africa we get clear examples of the diffusion of a linguistic feature over a large number of contiguous languages, e.g. tones, rich systems of noun classes, restricted tense–aspect choices in negative clauses, and (in one region) doubly articulated stops (where, for instance, the vocal organs close on a *g* and open on a *b*, as in the pronunciation of the language name Igbo). Africa has scarcely been looked at from the point of view of diffusion; at first glance it appears that there are a number of overlapping diffusion areas. (This is further discussed in §4.1.) And in the far south there is an additional diffusion area – overlapping with some of the others – characterised by the occurrence of clicks.

New Guinea shows the greatest concentration of languages in the world – at least 900 separate languages within a group of islands of less than 900,000 square kilometres (about the same area as Texas plus Oklahoma). Around 200 of these languages belong to the Austronesian family; the remainder divide between about 60 low-level families. There are a number of features that characterise New Guinea as a linguistic area, and others that apply across regions within it, e.g. head-marking clause structure; noun classes; impersonal verbs; medial verb structures; dual (and sometimes also trial or paucal) number in bound pronouns; neutralisation of the contrast between second and third person in non-singular numbers for pronouns. It may be possible to establish genetic relations between some of these low-level families, but only if areal and genetic similarities can be disentangled. It is first necessary to make a thorough study of linguistic areas within New Guinea (e.g. Foley 1986: 263–8), then to factor out similarities which appear to be due to diffusion, and finally to look for common genetic retentions from among non-diffused similarities.

Australia is perhaps the longest-established and most integrated linguistic area. It is characterised by a lack of fricatives; a rich set of contrasts by place of articulation (up to six); a nasal corresponding to every stop; up to four laterals; two rhotics; a three-term number system in free pronouns; indefinite pronouns also having interrogative sense; nominative–absolutive inflection for pronouns but absolutive–ergative for nouns; use of a special 'avoidance' language style in the presence of one of a class of 'taboo' relatives. There are other features which hold over smaller regions within the continent: switch-reference marking; systems of noun classes; a small set of inflecting verbs which enter into many compounds; and a head-marking system, with the verb including bound pronominals cross-referencing core arguments. The important point is that in almost every case a particular feature holds over a continuous geographical block of languages. The languages with the most individualistic structures tend to be on the coast, where some of the diffusional patterns have not yet had chance to reach. We shall discuss the Australian language situation further in (b) of §6.3.

3.1 What can diffuse

It is probably true to say that any aspect of human culture can be borrowed from one community to another. Sapir (1921: 205) said 'we know that myths, religious ideas, types of social organization, industrial devices, and other features of culture may spread from point to point, gradually making themselves at home in cultures to which they were at one time alien'. To this list we can add songs, ceremonies, political systems, marriage rules, the domestication of animals, and agriculture.

Language, as a cultural trait, is eminently open to diffusion (see Schmidt 1872). Which features diffuse tends to vary a good deal from one linguistic situation to another. A great deal more study is needed about which sorts of features are borrowed, and in what circumstances. It is, however, possible to put forward some tentative generalisations.

(a) *Phonetics and phonology*

People naturally tend to accommodate their habits of pronunciation to those of people they interact with, and this can extend to the creation of new phonological contrasts (or the loss of old ones). Prosodic and secondary contrasts such as tone, glottalisation, nasalisation, will typically diffuse. In most cases a new contrast will arise – to copy something that occurs in a neighbouring language – by internal change, rather than through the borrowing of forms. For instance, Indo-Aryan languages developed retroflexion (to be like Dravidian) by a series of changes that began with a retroflex sibilant and spread by assimilations, etc. (Masica 1991: 157ff.).

(b) *Lexemes*

The name in a contact language for a new tool or animal or idea may be taken over with that new thing. This is one kind of lexical borrowing. Another kind stems from the custom in some societies of tabooing the name of a dead person, and also vocabulary items that have a similar form to this name; these are often replaced by a lexeme from a neighbouring language.

The conditions for lexical borrowing vary greatly (and will be discussed further in §3.2) but, as a general rule, any lexeme may be borrowed (and may over time diffuse over a considerable area). In some parts of the world, core vocabulary (the most common words, referring to body parts, water, fire, mother, father, and the like) is borrowed less than non-core items; in other regions this restriction does not apply. In many situations nouns are borrowed more freely than verbs;[4] then, if two languages have a higher proportion of verbs in common than of nouns, this is a likely indication of close genetic relationship. However, the trait of nouns being borrowed more readily than verbs does not apply everywhere, and cannot be taken to be a general principle.[5]

(c) *Grammatical categories, construction types and techniques*[6]

The way in which a grammar is organised (but not the forms themselves) will always tend to be accommodated towards grammars of other languages of which some speakers have an active knowledge (and this will happen spontaneously, without any awareness of what is taking place).[7]

---

[4] There can be a number of reasons for this. One is that in many languages nouns are free forms (the root can occur with no affix, in citation and in one core syntactic function) whereas verbs are bound (the root is never used alone, but must take an affix from an inflectional system).

Breen (1990: 154–63) has examined the borrowability/genetic retentiveness of various types of words across a selection of Australian languages. His findings include: verbs are borrowed least often and names for fauna most often, with names for items of material culture coming between these extremes.

[5] For instance, Modern Russian borrows verbs as freely as it does nouns (Alexandra Aikhenvald, personal communication).

[6] Campbell (1993) discusses some universal tendencies for grammatical borrowing. These include: a language tends to borrow new constructions that are compatible with its overall pattern of grammatical organisation; and languages often borrow to fill gaps in their own grammatical systems.

[7] We also get calques, the loan translation of a phrase or compound word, preserving the grammar of the original language with a morpheme-by-morpheme translation of forms into the borrowing language. For instance, the modern English word *gospel* comes from Old English *gōd-spell* ('good-message') which was a calque from Greek *eu-angélion* ('good-message').

Perhaps the most common feature to diffuse is constituent order (often called just 'word order').[8] The literature abounds with examples of this, e.g. in most Semitic languages the verb is not in final position but those languages that moved into Ethiopia became verb-final, like the Cushitic languages they came into contact with there (Leslau 1945). Similarity in constituent order is among the worst possible types of evidence for genetic relationship, and the least useful feature to try to reconstruct for a proto-language.

A language may readily adapt its functional profile – whether head-marking or dependent-marking (Nichols 1986) – to that of language(s) with which it is in contact. Classifiers or noun class systems also readily diffuse – the fact of having such a system, not the forms themselves (which generally come from the language's internal resources). A system of switch-reference markers, or serial verb constructions, are also typically found in all the languages of a continuous region. (See, for instance, Austin 1981, on the areal distribution of switch-reference marking in Australia.)

The degree of diffusability of other types of categories and techniques (e.g. strategies for incorporation, nominalisation, relative clauses) is a topic which demands detailed investigation across all types of borrowing situations.

(d) Grammatical forms

There is again great variation between different parts of the world, but, by and large, grammatical forms are borrowed less readily than lexemes or grammatical categories. Still it does happen – Heath (1978) gives examples from the Arnhem Land region of Australia (e.g. borrowing of ablative suffix -*wala*, and of negative affix -*ʔmayʔ*). Sapir was of the opinion that grammatical forms are highly resistant to

---

[8] Another type of grammatical feature particularly open to borrowing is connectives. When a language without connectives such as 'or', 'and', 'until' and 'if' comes in contact with a language that has them, these can be amongst the first grammatical items to be borrowed.

borrowing and, as a result, similarity of grammatical forms is almost always indicative of genetic relationship. He suggested (1921: 203) that 'a really serious morphological influence is not, perhaps, impossible, but that its operation is so slow that it has hardly ever had the chance to incorporate itself in the relatively small portion of linguistic history that lies open to inspection'. It is true that during a family-tree-type expansion there is little opportunity for grammatical forms to be borrowed between contiguous languages. But during periods of linguistic equilibrium there was time a-plenty (perhaps tens of millennia) and then grammatical forms certainly were borrowed.

However, there are certain grammatical phenomena that are very unlikely to be borrowed, under any circumstances. These are:

(i) suppletions, such as *good/better/best* and *go/went*.
(ii) morphological irregularities, such as *sing/sang, bring/brought*.
(iii) complete paradigms, e.g. a pronoun paradigm, a noun declension or a verb conjugation.

Since these features are least liable to be borrowed, they are as a consequence the surest indicators of genetic relationship.

3.2 Languages in contact

There are two major questions to be asked about the possibilities for diffusion between two languages that are in contact: (a) who borrows from who; and (b) what gets borrowed. Taking these in turn:

(a) *Who borrows from who?*

There are two main factors here

(i) PRESTIGE There are polar possibilities. If two languages are of equal prestige in a community there is likely to be bilingualism in both directions (e.g. German and French in Luxemburg). But if language X has particular prestige – as the language of the ruling class, or the language of culture – then speakers of Y will acquire some competence in X but speakers of X are unlikely to understand or speak Y. In this case, Y will change to become more like X, and not the reverse.

(ii) COMPLEXITY   If language X is more complex than language Y, then speakers of X will find it easier to learn and speak Y, as a second language, than the other way round. (See the examples quoted at (c-iii) in Chapter 8.) In such a circumstance, X is likely to borrow from Y, and to get more like Y, but Y is less likely to change in the direction of X.

The complexity could be phonological, e.g. X may have complex syllable structure, say $C(C)V(C)(C)$, while Y has simply CV. Or grammatical, e.g. X may mark syntactic function mainly by bound pronominal elements in the verb while Y employs contrastive constituent order.

Sometimes it is not the actual relative simplicity that is the motivating factor, but rather speakers' perception of it. Randy LaPolla (personal communication) reports that, in a part of Yunnan China, where speakers of Nusu and Lisu live together, the Nusu people all learn Lisu but the Lisu seldom learn Nusu because they say it is too complicated and hard to learn (the Nusu speakers agree, and encourage this attitude). Actually, Nusu is no more complicated than Lisu.

Even if there is bilingualism in each direction we may have a marked directionality of influence. As Weinreich stated, in his classic study (1953: 41): 'significantly, in the interference of two grammatical patterns it is ordinarily the one which uses relatively free and invariant morphemes in its paradigm – one might say, the more explicit pattern – which serves as the model for imitation. This seems to be true not only in the creation of new categories . . . but also in those cases where a new set of formants is developed to fulfil a pre-existing grammatical function.' (He follows this with illustrative examples.)[9]

---

[9] Similar work has been done by Heath (1978) on investigating conditions under which grammatical forms may be borrowed in a part of Australia.

Another factor concerns the kind of items that are available to be borrowed. If group A comes into contact with group B, and A has certain artefacts, customs and activities that B lacks, then B is likely to borrow the names of these from A. Generally, the group with the greatest prestige will be the one with the most new things and the non-prestige language will borrow from it, e.g. Australian Aboriginal languages have borrowed, from English, terms for 'gun', 'pub', 'church', 'policeman', 'car', 'shirt', 'trousers', 'mirror', 'work', 'buy' and 'muster'. But when a prestige language is an invader, it may borrow terms from the indigenous languages for local flora, fauna and artefacts; witness loan words in English from Australian languages such as *kangaroo, wombat, budgerigar* and *boomerang*.

(b) What gets borrowed?

Over and above the general principles concerning what linguistic features are most open to borrowing, summarised in §3.1, social and linguistic attitudes determine what happens in any particular instance.

People tend to think of their language in terms of its dictionary (the open classes of noun, verb, adjective). They identify it with the lexicon and attempt to control this as an indicator of ethnic identity. They are not in the same way aware of grammatical categories (or forms) and are scarcely aware of changes that may take place in this area.

Aikhenvald (1996) describes the Vaupés River basin, on the Colombia/Brazil border, where each person must marry someone from another language group. As one speaker put it: 'those who speak the same language as us are like brothers, and we do not marry our sisters'. This leads to rampant multilingualism. Interestingly, there have been almost no lexical borrowings. People take particular care not to mix languages, and for them a language is its dictionary. There has, however, been tremendous grammatical diffusion. Tariana (from the Arawak family) is a non-prestige language in the Vaupés region and has adopted many features from the prestige Tucanoan languages. These include switch-reference marking and verb compounding. Tariana has remodelled its modality, tense–aspect and evidentiality systems, to be more similar to those in Tucanoan. (All of these changes involve the organisation of the grammar; no grammatical forms have been borrowed.) Tariana has also developed two new vowel phonemes (high unrounded central *i* and mid back *o*) to produce a system more like Tucanoan. There is even a change in progress where vowel length is being replaced by pitch accent, to accord more nearly with the tone system in Tucanoan.

There are similar examples from other parts of the world. In Gumperz and Wilson's classic study (1971) of the Indian village, Kupwar, they find that local varieties of Kannada (Dravidian) and of Marathi and Urdu (Indo-Aryan) have converged on a single syntactic structure and similar morphological systems, but maintain distinct lexical and grammatical forms.[10]

Sapir (1921: 196) gave another example: 'the Athabaskan languages of America are spoken by people that have had astonishingly varied cultural contacts, yet nowhere do we find that an Athabaskan dialect has borrowed at all freely from a neighbouring language. These languages have always found it easier to create new words by compounding afresh elements ready to hand. They have for this reason been highly resistant to receiving the linguistic impress of the external cultural experiences of their speakers.'

There may be a partial linguistic reason for the lack of borrowing by Athabaskan languages; the structures are complex, with mostly bound forms, so that it would be difficult to assign a foreign form to an Athabaskan root. But it is undoubtedly partly a matter of attitude. Some people, it seems, just do not want to borrow lexemes, but prefer to create names for new things from language-internal resources.

---

[10] Another seminal study is that of Nadkarni (1975), discussing how the relative clause construction in Kannada, a Dravidian language, is replacing the native relative clause construction in Konkani, an Indo-Aryan language, in a contact situation.

Such languages are probably in a minority. In many cases of contact we do find lexical borrowing at a steady rate, and borrowing of grammatical forms at a much slower rate. This applies in most (but not all) parts of Australia. It is partly motivated by the need to replace words tabooed due to similarity to the name of a dead relative,[11] but partly by a general openness to take over words from neighbouring languages. Aborigines do identify with their languages, but they talk in terms of differences in certain critical lexemes (or words like 'this' and 'that'), not of the whole lexicon.[12]

We thus have – in Australia – an interesting situation. If two languages come into contact and there is little vocabulary in common, they will gradually borrow in both directions and this figure will rise until it reaches about 50%, where it will stabilise. And if one tribal group splits into two, with the result that what were two dialects develop (as mutual intelligibility is lost) into distinct languages, X and Y, they will at first have a high percentage of vocabulary in common (70% or so). As vocabulary is replaced, separately in each language, so the percentage of shared vocabulary will reduce. If a word is tabooed in X, a new form is unlikely to be taken from Y, since that language probably has the same original form as X, but rather from some other neighbouring language. The common vocabulary will gradually drop, until it reaches the equilibrium level of about

---

[11] Examples are in Dixon (1980: 98–9, 151). The tabooing can extend to loan words. Around 1980 a man called *Jack* died and members of his community (speakers of the Western Desert language) tabooed the word *cheque* (as in *social security cheque*). While the taboo lasted, the word *letter* was used in its place (Gloria Brennan, personal communication).

[12] When I began fieldwork in Australia in 1963, my Aboriginal teacher Chloe Grant explained that there were two tribes in her region and characterised them as follows: Jirrbal say *bana* for 'water' and *buni* for 'fire' but Girramay use *gamu* for 'water' and *yugu* for 'fire'. Closer study showed that these are mutually intelligible dialects of one language (in the linguistic sense of the term), sharing about 80% of their lexicon and with very similar grammar. But speakers identify tribal affiliation in terms of a few lexemes that differ, such as 'water' and 'fire' in this instance.

50%.[13] Thus, if two contiguous languages in Australia share about 50% vocabulary it is impossible – from this figure – to decide whether or not they are closely genetically related. In this circumstance one can look at the percentage of (a) verbs in common (if more than 50% this suggests a close genetic relationship and if less than 50% the lack of one) and (b) grammatical forms in common (a close genetic connection will be marked by a high proportion of shared grammatical forms, including paradigms). Within the Australian linguistic area, verbs tend to be replaced more slowly than other lexemes, and grammatical forms still more slowly.

The detailed argumentation underlying the 'rising to' or 'falling to' a 50% lexical equilibrium level will be found in Dixon (1972: 331–7).[14]

In summary, grammatical categories and techniques are always likely to diffuse, but in some contact situations we find – for a variety of reasons – that lexemes are scarcely borrowed, whereas in other situations they are freely borrowed. Over time, a people's attitude towards borrowing can change. A given language may be averse to borrowing from other languages for a period of some hundreds or thousands of years, but then it may change and begin borrowing in profusion. Japanese has been through stages like this (see Loveday 1996). The two stages have applied in reverse order in Hungarian; there were many borrowings but then, at a later stage, these were replaced by language-internal compounds or derivations.

[13] It is important to note that 50% vocabulary in common (and 70–80% grammar) does not make for 50% intelligibility. There would be little intelligibility in such a situation (although, of course, it is relatively easy to learn to speak and understand a language which has this degree of similarity to one's own).

[14] Alpher and Nash (ms. 1996) suggest that the actual equilibrium level should be less than 50%. However, the fact remains that most Australian languages do have a 50% vocabulary score with at least one neighbouring language, supporting the ideas put forward here, and the notion that the continent is a long-standing diffusion area.

4 The family tree model

There has been a persistent tendency in linguistics to take one idea (which could never be more than part of the whole picture) and to overapply it. This is evident in most recent grammatical theories. And it certainly applies to the branching family tree model for linguistic splitting and relationship.

In the ideal family tree situation we get one original language splitting into a small number of daughter languages (in the best instance, two), each of these in turn splitting into a small number of daughter languages, and so on. This model was developed for the Indo-European family and is broadly applicable to it. There are, however, a number of less than ideal features of the IE family tree. The first is that we appear to need a primary split into ten branches – it has not been possible to reach any consensus on further articulation within this ten. That a single ancestor language should split simultaneously into ten daughters is unlikely. (In §7 we shall examine an alternative scenario.) There is also the difficulty that some languages cannot be assigned a clear place within the tree; for instance, Singhalese is acknowledged to belong to the Indo-Aryan branch, but it cannot be assigned to any specific node within this branch.

Work on Indo-European is, by and large, of the highest quality and has acquired a justified prestige. (Add to this the fact that the IE languages themselves include the major prestige languages in the world today.) As a result the family tree is the 'received model' of linguistic relationship which scholars working in other areas attempt to apply to their own groups of languages. Sometimes the family tree model is applicable, and a genetic relationship can be proved in the same way that it has been for IE, e.g. Uralic, Semitic, Algonquian.

But in other instances a family-tree-type diagram has been posited without the right sort of proof, or any prospect that this could be provided.

A main thesis of this essay is that the family tree model, while appropriate and useful in many circumstances, is not applicable everywhere and cannot explain every type of relationship between languages. We need a more inclusive model, which integrates together the ideas of family tree and of diffusion area.

Proto-Indo-European is considered to have been spoken about 6,000 years ago; there are today over 100 IE languages. But human language is thought to have evolved at least 100,000 years in the past (many specialists would give an earlier figure). Suppose there was one original language, proto-Human (this question will be more fully discussed in §5.3). There are about 17 periods of 6,000 years in a 100,000 year span. If IE-type splitting were the norm (one language having 100 descendants after 6,000 years), proto-Human should by now have spawned $10^{2 \times 17} = 10^{34}$, or 10 million billion billion billion, languages; in fact we have about 5,000. (An even larger figure, 10^{60}, would be obtained by taking as a model the Austronesian family where one language has spawned over 1,000 daughters in a time span suggested to be no more than 5,000 years.) If we adopted a more modest rate of splitting, supposing that a language is likely to split into two languages every 6,000 years, we would expect proto-Human to have given rise to 2^{17}, or about 130,000, modern languages. If we allow for a number of languages becoming extinct along the way, this would be a more reasonable number. But note the assumption involved – a language splits into two about every 6,000 years. This is something of a totally different magnitude from what we know has happened in some parts of the world during recent centuries – for instance, the development of separate languages in the Romance and Indo-Aryan subgroups of IE, where we do have available a depth of written record.

The lesson from these calculations is that language split and expansion on the scale that is put forward for the IE and

Austronesian families is highly unusual. This sort of thing would have happened rather seldom in the history of human language. It should certainly not be taken as the only model for language development. For Austronesian there is a straightforward explanation for at least part of this mammoth split – expansion into the Pacific Islands was into previously unoccupied territory. In the case of IE we simply have an aggressive and imperialistic race, spreading and conquering. (Note how, during the past few centuries, English, Spanish and Portuguese have almost entirely replaced the indigenous languages in the Americas and in Australia; well over 1,000 languages are either dead or dying.)

I shall suggest below that the family tree model is only applicable during a period of punctuation, and not during periods of linguistic equilibrium. Language development during the past 100,000 and more years has involved long periods of equilibrium, with only the occasional punctuation.

4.1 Criteria

A family tree diagram, with X at the top and A,B,C, . . . along the bottom, states that A,B,C, . . . developed from X, by a number of language splits. There is one and only one way to prove such a claim: (a) to reconstruct the phonological system, at least several hundred lexemes (covering all areas of vocabulary) and parts of the grammatical system (pronouns, demonstratives, interrogatives and some affixes) for the postulated proto-language, X; and then (b) to describe the systematic processes of change by which X developed into each of the daughter languages A,B,C, . . .

There exists the comparative method, a quasi-procedure for reconstruction. Applied in an intelligent way, this will in most cases suggest a plausible proto-system.[1] (However the comparative

---

[1] But note Bloomfield's caveat (1933: 318): 'The comparative method, then – our only method for the reconstruction of prehistoric language – would work accu-

method is by no means fool-proof; it is not a discovery procedure, an algorithm that can be applied mechanically to provide a reconstruction. The appendix discusses cases in which – applied as a discovery procedure – it would yield the wrong result.)

In fact, *the way in which* a linguistic characterisation of a proto-language is arrived at is essentially irrelevant. It could have been obtained by fairly strict application of the comparative method, or it could have been suggested by a linguist intuitively (or it could even have come to them in a dream). The only point at issue is that a description of a good part of the proto-language should be provided, such that the systems of modern languages can be derived from it by a series of plausible, systematic changes.

The genetic relationship of IE languages, in a family tree model, has of course been eminently proved by this criterion. Proof has also been provided – or is being provided – for some other language families. But for many groups of languages that have been posited to comprise a language family, no serious attempt has been made to reconstruct part of the system of a proto-language, nor does it seem likely that it will prove possible to do so.

Often we find that the ideas of 'genetic relationship' and 'language family' are conceived of in a quite different way from those described above. But then these terms are used as if they were equivalent in sense to the same terms used in the context of IE or other families for which the criterion of proof for genetic relationship has been met.

There are three main strands of such work – typological, lexicostatistic and 'Nostratic'. We discuss these in turn.

(a) Based on typological features

Typically, a number of typological features are quoted, in which a group of languages concur, and this is taken as evidence of genetic connection. For example, Shibatani (1990: 94–118) surveys the

> rately for absolutely uniform speech-communities and sudden, sharp cleavages.
> Since these presuppositions are never fully realised, the comparative method
> cannot claim to picture the historical process.'

suggestions for a genetic relationship between Japanese and various other groups of languages. These include Fujioka (1908) who presented 'fourteen characteristic features of Ural-Altaic languages' that also apply to Japanese. It will suffice here to quote just four (the first and every fourth after that): '(a) no consonant sequences occur in word-initial position; ... (e) there is no grammatical gender distinction; ... (j) postpositions, instead of prepositions, are used; ... (n) conjunctions are not used widely.' But all of these are characteristics which diffuse. Careful examination indicates that the established families, Turkic, Mongolian and Tungusic, form a linguistic area (called Altaic) and that some features are also shared with the Uralic family. These typological similarities with Japanese may possibly be due to areal influence; or they may be coincidental. (Many languages, from other parts of the world, do share these features.)

There has been no successful attempt to reconstruct a linguistic system for 'proto-Altaic' or 'proto-Uralic-Altaic' or 'proto-Uralic-Altaic-Japanese(-Korean)', and the ways in which the modern languages have developed from such a proto-system. Sufficient criteria have not been given that would justify talking of a genetic relationship here. We simply have typological similarities, which is a totally different matter.

Africa is linguistically fascinating, with well over 1,000 languages, many of them showing dauntingly complex structures. A number have been well described but for many languages we have very little published data. About 1,000 languages have been grouped together in a putative 'Niger-Congo family', suggested by Greenberg (1963). One finds statements like '[Greenberg's] major conclusions have by now become the prevailing orthodoxy for most scholars' (Williamson 1989: 8). However, one searches in vain for proof of this 'genetic relationship'. Africanists tend to respond to queries about this matter from outsiders by saying that only Africanists can judge such matters. Maybe. But after reviewing the available literature an outsider is forced to conclude that the idea of genetic relationship and the term 'language family' are used in quite different ways by

Africanists and by scholars working on languages from other parts of
the world.

Common features quoted in support of 'Niger-Congo' are
systems of tones, and of noun classes (or genders). Note, though, that
not every Niger-Congo language has even these two characteristics.
Greenberg (1963: 10) states: 'while the presence of these [noun class]
affixes is important evidence for affiliation with the Niger-Congo
family, absence of the affixes does not prove lack of connection'.
(Noun classes are absent from the putative Mande subgroup, for
instance.) Greenberg's establishment of 'Niger-Congo' was based on
what he calls 'mass comparison', inspecting the forms of lexemes in a
sample of languages for apparent similarities. Nowhere is the full set
of data given – just a sample of seven words in eight languages
(Greenberg 1963: 4). It is true that there are some formal similarities
between the affixes that mark noun classes – but these are prefixes in
some languages and suffixes in others. Greenberg suggests, plausibly,
that they may have developed from demonstratives.

Other features mentioned as characteristics for 'Niger-Congo'
include: CVCV root structure; -CV shape for suffixes; vowel
harmony; nasal-plus-stop sequences or else prenasalised stops; verb
serialisation; and either subject-object-verb or subject-verb-object
constituent order (Williamson 1989: 20ff.). Like tones and noun
classes these are all features which recur in other parts of the world
and they are all eminently open to diffusion. Noun class affixes themselves are not too likely to be borrowed, but they are said to come
from demonstratives and these are more likely to diffuse.

The hypothesis of a 'Niger-Congo family' was first put forward
almost fifty years ago. During the intervening period no attempt has
been made to prove this hypothesis by the criteria used for IE, Uralic,
Algonquian, etc. In fact, as mentioned in §3, it appears that Sub-
Saharan Africa is characterised by an overlapping series of diffusion
areas (for those features that are generally taken as indicative of
genetic relationship).

This is not to deny that some genetic groupings may be

establishable within this linguistic area. Some have been (e.g. the Bantu languages) and others undoubtedly will be. But any hypothesis of relationship must be proved – by reconstructing a good deal of the linguistic system of a proto-language, and by detailing the systematic changes by which modern languages developed from this. Plainly, the first task is to try to reconstruct proto-languages for some of the lower nodes on the 'Niger-Congo family tree', and then see if it is possible to work further from these. And it should always be borne in mind that there are several possible reasons for any similarities between languages – genetic retention, areal diffusion, or just chance typological similarity.

The Niger-Congo situation is a classic example of taking the IE-type family tree as the only model of linguistic relationship, and employing it willy-nilly, without proper care and criteria.

More recently, Greenberg (1987) has applied the same method of 'mass comparison' to the Americas, and purports to have 'proved' the genetic relationships between several dozen distinct families and many language isolates. This time he has published a part of the data base, and his original notebooks are on file. It has been pointed out that (i) Greenberg had finalised his scheme of relationships before he began assembling the data; and (ii) much of the data is incorrect,[2] being taken either from a different language to that indicated or else from old sources that are not phonetically reliable (passing over more modern sources that are reliable). (See, among other critiques, Chafe 1987, Campbell 1988, Adelaar 1989, Goddard 1990, Rankin 1992, Kimball 1992, and Berman 1992).[3]

In the Americas (particularly in North America) one does have

---

[2] Greenberg (1989: 112) stated 'although I have exercised great care, it would be miraculous if, handling such a vast amount of material, there were no errors of fact or interpretation'. Adelaar (1989: 253), a specialist on Quechua, responded: 'if one looks at the quality of the data Greenberg presents ... the number of erroneous forms probably exceeds that of the correct forms'.

[3] There is also Greenberg's 'Indo-Pacific hypothesis' (1971) purporting to show that the 60-odd Papuan families from New Guinea, the extinct languages of

extensive data available, much of it of high quality, and a tradition of establishing genetic relationships using the same criteria as those employed in the IE field. Greenberg's work on the languages of the Americas does not employ established criteria for establishing genetic relationships and is transparently inadequate.[4] It is also rather like the clock that strikes thirteen– not only is it implausible in itself but it casts doubt on all that has gone before. That is, it has made some people (including me) go back and look at the 'mass comparison' method as applied to African languages, and perceive its limitations. But at least 'Niger-Congo' does have some of the characteristics of a linguistic area, which is more than can be said of the Americas. And it is likely that some parts of the putative 'Niger-Congo family tree' will be proved to have genetic unity, whereas few or none of the links Greenberg suggests between the established language families and isolates in the Americas are ever likely to be proved.

(b) *Lexicostatistics and glottochronology*

Swadesh (1951) put forward a magical formula for establishing 'genetic' relationships. There would no longer be any need to spend decades compiling grammars and dictionaries, then looking for systematic correspondences and working on reconstruction. One

Tasmania, and the various languages spoken in the Andaman Islands are genetically related. He offers eleven grammatical criteria; only one of which is satisfied by Tasmanian. Of the eighty-four lexical items listed, putative Tasmanian cognates are mentioned for less than one quarter; none of them is convincing. This idea lacks any substance, and is perhaps even more fanciful than Greenberg's American Indian work.

[4] Matisoff (1990: 107) comments that Greenberg's work on American languages 'is only the tip of the iceberg. We are promised another book shortly . . . that will prove that Indo-European itself belongs to a much vaster language family called "Eurasiatic", which includes Japanese, Ural-Altaic and Eskimo-Aleut. For many linguists, such views fall more into the category of religious beliefs than scientifically testable hypotheses, about on a par with claims that : "all languages have the same underlying deep structure" and "the position of the stars at the moment of our birth determines our character".

simply gathered a specified 100- (or perhaps 200-) word list of core vocabulary in each of a number of languages and compared them, noting – by inspection – how many items appeared to be cognate between these core vocabularies. Then a formula told you how the languages were related (Lexicostatistics) and also the time-depth of their common proto-language (Glottochronology). Together with this method came an array of new terminology. The term 'language family' was used with a quite new sense, for languages sharing 36–81% of core vocabulary. We also had 'stock', 'microphylum', 'mesophylum' and 'macrophylum' (here the cognate percentage is less than 1%!) (Gudschinsky 1956).

Like all short cuts, this didn't work. It was based on illicit assumptions – that one can infer genetic relationships from lexicon alone; that the lexicon of all languages is always replaced at a constant rate; and that core vocabulary always behaves in a different way from non-core. There were (for some people) a few mad, happy years of 100-word list comparison before lexicostatistics was decisively discredited (see Bergslund and Vogt 1962; and also Hoijer 1956, Arndt 1959, Teeter 1963, Campbell 1977: 63–5, Embleton 1992).[5]

[5] Lexicostatistics and glottochronology are still practised in a few odd corners of the world (including Russia, where these methods were introduced in the 1980s, twenty years after being discarded by serious linguistics in the West). I am sorry to have to report that one of these corners is in Australia. The first draft of my general survey of Australian languages (published as Dixon 1980) included a couple of pages on why the lexicostatistical classification should be regarded with distrust. John Lyons was the publisher's academic editor for the volume and he recommended this discussion be shortened, since – he believed – all linguists were by then familiar with the shortcomings of lexicostatistics and glottochronology. I took his advice. But Lyons wasn't aware that the news about lexicostatistics had not (and still has not) reached some Australianists.

The most recent piece of work along these lines is by McConvell, who had previously published excellent studies on descriptive and historical topics in Australian linguistics. Quoting Ussher (who by adding up the dates in the Bible decided that the world was created in 4004 BC), McConvell (1996) gives specific dates for intermediate nodes on a putative family tree against which he invites archaeologists to calibrate their results. He states: 'O'Grady argues that on the basis of standard glottochronology, Pama-Nyungan would be assigned an age of

Comparison of core vocabularies is not, of course, a useless exercise. It is a very helpful first step when dealing with new languages and may suggest hypotheses about possible relationships which can be an aid in planning detailed descriptive and comparative work. But it should never be taken as proof of genetic relationships. (Sometimes lexicostatistics results do correlate well with what is proved by careful comparison and reconstruction, but in other circumstances they do not.)

A number of genetic groups and subgroups were put forward on the basis of lexicostatistical comparison. Although lexicostatistics has been long discredited, some people still work in terms of these genetic groups – they should be proved, according to proper criteria, or else discarded (e.g. the 'Pama-Nyungan subgroup' in Australia).

(c) 'Nostratic'

If the family tree model is all one has, there is a temptation to apply it, apply it again, and yet again. Why stop? A number of language families have been firmly established (or are in the process of being established); why not attempt to relate them together, into a higher-level family tree?

Pedersen (1931: 334–9) surveyed opinions that IE might be related to Semitic (and thus, presumably, to the rest of Afroasiatic); and/or to Uralic; perhaps to Turkic, Mongolian and Tungusic; perhaps to Eskimo; perhaps to some of the Caucasian families; perhaps to Basque. He suggested: 'as a comprehensive designation for the families of languages which are related to Indo-European, we

about 8000 years, but that a more realistic figure would be about half that (4000 BP) because of accelerated lexical change in Australia due to such factors as lexical taboo'. McConvell says he is 'convinced' it 'is much more like 6000 years old than 40,000 years or even 12,000 years'. Dixon (forthcoming) explains why the Pama-Nyungan typological group should not be assigned genetic status, and why all questions about time depth within the Australian linguistic area can have only one honest answer: 'we don't know'.

may employ the expression Nostratian Languages (from Latin *nostrās* "our countryman")'.

During recent years this term has been revived by a group of mainly Russian scholars (and modified to 'Nostratic') to cover a putative linkage of language families – IE, Uralic, Turkic, Mongolian, Tungusic,[6] Dravidian, South Caucasian (Kartvelian) and perhaps Afroasiatic (opinions vary on this[7]). These 'Nostraticists' purport to work in terms of the comparative method, by assembling cognate sets. However, they achieve their results only by allowing excessive phonological and semantic leeway. In the 'reconstructions', scarcely any vowels are specified (given just as V), N is often employed for an unspecified nasal, and so on.

It is of course perfectly reasonable to look for possible links between established language families – Collinder (1965: 30–4) has some useful observations about the possibility of a connection between Uralic and IE. But one should always proceed a step at a time. To suddenly link together seven (or eight) families is more than a little implausible, especially when, for some of them (Dravidian, Afroasiatic), the proto-language of that family still needs considerable work.[8] The 'Nostraticists' do not stop here. There have also been

---

[6] Turkic, Mongolian and Tungusic have often been taken to make up a larger family, Altaic. However, most experts on these languages now believe their similarities to be largely areal (see, for instance, Baldi 1990: 477–561).

[7] Some Nostraticists consider Afroasiatic to be a family within Nostratic; others have Afroasiatic as a family on a par with Nostratic, and genetically linked to it within Nostratic–Afroasiatic.

[8] These language families have been recognised for a considerable period of time and no scholar has been able to prove (to the satisfaction of the entire academic community) that any two of them are genetically related. But the Moscow Nostraticists put forward a genetic relationship between *all* of them on the basis of just a few years' work.

   Such a scenario – that a proof has been obtained, all at once, of the higher-level relationship of seven or eight well-established families – is simply implausible. It is rather like someone reporting that the Queen of England moonlights as a door-to-door encyclopaedia salesperson (which is why she declines all invitations to dinner parties). One would simply pay no attention at all to such a

suggestions of genetic units Eskimo-Nostratic ('cognate' sets include
proto-Eskimo *mac(j)a* and proto-Nostratic **mV[ź]V* 'sun'), Sino-
Tibetan plus North-east and North-west Caucasian (Sino-
Caucasian), Na-Dene plus North-east and North-west Caucasian;
and then Nostratic plus Sino-Caucasian. (See, for instance,
Shevoroshkin and Manaster Ramer 1991.) And so on. Why stop?[9]

It is relevant to enquire how this Nostratic idea came to be
accepted as an orthodoxy in a country like Russia which has such
high standards in other scientific fields (physics and mathematics, for
example). The Nostratic idea took root at a time when Russian intel-
lectuals were cut off from close contact with the rest of the world, in
a sort of Lord-of-the-Flies situation; there was no peer group available that would have employed proper standards of scientific assessment and demonstrated the unsound basis of the idea.

The Russian Nostraticists openly boasted (and still boast) that
they are cleverer than anyone who has come before, which was why
they were able to relate many families together, all at once, something
that had not previously been achieved. 'In fact, however, sober-
minded scholars have shrunk from megalocomparisons not because

suggestion; it is, from our knowledge of the world in which we live, palpable
poppycock.

    Some respected scholars have paid attention to the details of the proposal
and, as expected, the initial reaction that it must be nonsensical is borne out. In
many cases the basic word forms used are erroneous; the methodology of the
comparative method is stretched way beyond its limits, allowing a wide latitude
in phonological and semantic 'correspondences'; and the 'reconstructions' are
selective and incomplete. (See, for instance, Campbell, forthcoming-a, and many
further references therein.)

[9] The Nostraticists are also guilty of an error of axiom. They have put forward the
idea that the main thing to be considered when formulating a genetic connection
between two languages is lexemes. Yet every proponent of the comparative
method – from Meillet on down – emphasises the primary importance of establishing correspondences between grammatical forms, preferably between
grammatical paradigms (see, for instance, Nichols 1996). This is the principle
on which the genetic proofs of Indo-European, Uralic, South Caucasian and
Dravidian are based. Yet the Nostraticists assign quite different priorities in
positing higher-level relationships.

they are so difficult, but because they are so easy. When the number of languages being considered is so large, when their relationship (if any) is remote, and the criteria for sound correspondences are lax, it is not very hard to find "phono-semantic lookalikes" – forms which more or less resemble each other both in sound and in meaning' (Matisoff 1990: 109–10).

The methods of comparative linguistics are such that, if criteria which should be strictly maintained are relaxed, just a little, it is possible to prove – literally – that anything is related to everything. Swadesh (1960) purported to establish genetic connections between a number of distinct language families in Central America by permitting generous phonological and semantic correspondences, similar to the Nostraticists. Longacre (1961) and Olmsted (1961) provided admirable critiques of the method and results. And then Callaghan and Miller (1962) demonstrated that, with regular 'cognate sets' just as valid as those used by Swadesh, English can be shown to be a 'Macro-Mixtecan' language. For example they connected the form *yute* 'comb' in proto-Macro-Mixtecan with *head* in English, and *yeti-ni* or *yeyet-ni* 'skin' with English *hide*, 'demonstrating' correspondences *y:h* and *t:d*. Their point was that, with the sort of semantic and phonological latitude which Swadesh allowed himself, it can be 'shown' that any language is related to Macro-Mixtecan (or to any other family).

The error in all this work is not just in failing to take proper scientific care in comparing languages, but in relying on family trees as the only model of linguistic relationship. Within an integrated model of linguistic relationships (combining the family tree and diffusion models) and with a clearer idea of the difficulties involved in the idea of 'proto-language', there could be no temptation to perpetrate anything such as 'Nostratic'.

In summary, there are many situations where the family tree model is appropriate, and can be proved through reconstruction of a significant part of the linguistic system of a proto-language, together with the systematic changes that have given rise to the modern languages. But such cases must be carefully distinguished from situations in which we just have typological similarities.

Whether a genetic connection between languages is provable depends on a number of factors, including the morphological type of the languages concerned and the average length of forms. A cognate set between polysyllabic forms provides much better evidence than one involving monosyllables, or single-segment forms. If the verb 'go' is *-gimlar-* in two languages, this is a stronger evidence of relationship than if it were *-a-*. For a group of languages where many roots consist of a single consonant (such as North-west Caucasian) reconstruction is more problematic than where most roots are polysyllabic (e.g. Uralic).

Languages can be roughly classed into three types: isolating, where each meaning element makes up a distinct word (e.g. Vietnamese and Chinese); agglutinative, where a word is likely to contain several meaning elements but these are clearly separable (e.g. Turkish and Swahili); and fusional, where a word will contain several meaning elements some of them being fused together, so that a single vowel may simultaneously mark, say, tense, voice, and person and number of subject (e.g. Latin and Sanskrit).

Proof of genetic relationship rests heavily on grammatical elements, including affixes. The ideal situation is to have a proto-language that is agglutinative[10] and modern languages that vary from agglutinative to fusional. If a group of modern languages are all basically isolating, with few grammatical affixes, it may never be possible to prove genetic connection with the same degree of confidence as for an agglutinative group.

As languages change over time, they tend – very roughly – to

---

[10] Proto-Indo-European had a fairly fusional structure (with ablaut and stress shift). This structure can be reconstructed because these fusional features have been retained in many of the descendants (and here we are fortunate in having old records).

move around a typological circle: isolating to agglutinating, to fusional, back to isolating, and so on. If we place the isolating type at the four o'clock position, agglutinative at eight o'clock and fusional at twelve o'clock, around a clock-face, it is possible to describe recent movements in various language families. Proto-Indo-European was at about twelve o'clock but modern branches of the family have moved, at different rates, towards a more isolating position (some to one or two o'clock, others towards three o'clock). Early Chinese is thought to have been at about three o'clock, Classical Chinese was a fairly pure isolating type at four o'clock, while Modern Chinese languages are acquiring a mildly agglutinative structure, towards five o'clock. Proto-Dravidian was on the isolating side of agglutinative, at about seven o'clock, and modern Dravidian languages have moved around the cycle towards nine o'clock. Proto-Finno-Ugric may have been at around nine o'clock, with modern languages moving to ten or eleven o'clock (Dixon 1994: 183–5). For Egyptian, which has a long recorded history, Hodge (1970) describes how it moved right around the cycle, from fusional back again to fusional, over a period of about 3,000 years.[11]

Modern-day isolating languages may have had a fusional ancestor, whose portmanteau morphemes have been lost through phonological and morphological change;[12] it may never be possible to reconstruct even an outline of what the shape of the proto-language was like. Present-day agglutinative languages may have had an ancestor of more isolating profile, with what were distinct words having developed into grammatical affixes (e.g. postpositions into cases). The Dravidian family is roughly of this type and here one

[11] Other useful discussions include Matisoff (1976) and DeLancey (1985).

[12] Languages of the Tai-Kadai family are isolating, but there are semantically related sets of words – both between languages and within languages – that have the appearance of being related through something like ablaut (Li 1977: 38–41, and Tony Diller, personal communication). These suggest that the proto-language may have had a fusional character.

can successfully recover a good deal of the proto-language. If the proto-language was agglutinative then many or most of its modern descendants are likely to have merged grammatical morphemes into a more fusional structure; reconstructing the original morphemes is not likely to be an easy task, but – depending on the types of fusion in individual languages and on how much agglutination is still evident in some modern languages – a measure of success may be achieved.

The caveat is that in none of these cases can we be certain that we have achieved the correct result. If a group of modern languages are all isolating, the proto-language could also have been isolating; or it could have been fusional. And if there is no absolute certainty about the type of language we are attempting to reconstruct, this throws an element of doubt over every detail of the putative reconstruction.

Specialists in related disciplines take great interest in the family tree diagrams put forward by linguists. Archaeologists, geneticists and anthropologists like to be given a clear-cut linguistic hypothesis, about where and when a proto-language was spoken and exactly how it split and spread. They happily accept any family tree that is produced, without stopping to ask whether it is soundly based, and whether it is accepted by the majority of linguists. The excesses of Greenberg and the 'Nostraticists' have thus received acceptance outside linguistics itself. And also in newspapers, where 'proto-World' is a news item while 'there are more than 200 language families in the world, with little prospect of providing higher-level genetic links between them' goes straight into the trash bin.

A credulous media – especially the popular science magazines and science programs on TV – have embraced the most crackpot ideas about language relationships, even encouraging their proponents to speak a sentence or two in 'proto-World'! As a result, the public gains a distorted idea of what real linguists do, and of what linguistics, as a science, is capable of proving. There is no reputable historical linguist,[13] anywhere in the world, who accepts the claims of Greenberg and the Nostraticists. Yet, scarcely any have taken time away from their academic pursuits to draw to the public's attention the facts about what language relationships can be scientifically proved. The results of historical linguistics may not be spectacular, but this is no reason for ignoring them in favour of spectacular – but vacuous – speculations.

When linguists tell archaeologists and geneticists that such and such a putative family tree is without scientific basis, the response is 'give us another family tree to replace it then.' If the linguists answer that the family tree model may not be applicable for the groups of languages in question – that it is a matter of typological similarity and linguistic area – the non-linguists may turn away with a shrug (and will probably continue using the unjustified family tree, just because they consider they need something like this, to tie their archaeological and genetic theories to).[14]

This is an outside pressure that linguists have to resist. We must set out to prove whatever genetic relationships can be proved, but we must take care not to suggest family trees where no reconstruction has been attempted or is likely to be possible. And we must educate people outside our profession both about the different kinds of relationships that are found between languages, and that the family tree is just one model, which is only applicable in certain situations.

---

[13] Lest this be thought circular, let me provide a criterion for recognising a large group of reputable historical linguists: anyone who teaches the subject at a leading university in the USA or in an EEC nation.

[14] If the punctuated equilibrium model, put forward in this essay, does have validity, it follows that archaeologists and geneticists should pay attention to the idea of equilibrium periods in framing their own hypotheses. Indeed, there are recent signs that they may be starting to do so.

4.2 Proto-languages

A natural language is rather like an old garment that has been patched and mended. The overall outline is perceivable, to a greater or lesser extent, but some parts have worn away and been replaced, one section may have been lost altogether, and in another place a bit from another source may have been tacked on. In contrast, a proto-language – as it is generally reconstructed – resembles a garment straight from the factory, every button in place, every zip working, every seam sewn neatly and evenly.

That is to say, a natural language is likely to have suppletions and irregularities of inflection in its grammar, and one or more sub-strata/superstrata in lexicon and perhaps also in grammar and phonology. Yet many proto-languages, as they are reconstructed, are regular and homogeneous. It is often said that this is the nature of the comparative method – that one cannot do otherwise. It is agreed by most (but not by all) historical linguists that a reconstructed proto-language can be, at best, an *approximation* to what the putative unique ancestor of a given language family may have been like.

It follows from this that comparing the reconstructed proto-languages of established linguistic families, to see whether there is any higher-level genetic connection between them, is a highly speculative venture. One is comparing systems that may correspond, to some extent, to just some part of what the actual ancestor language was like.

Consider present-day English. Suppose that at some time in the future linguists try to reconstruct English, on the basis of a number of latter-day descendant languages (with no direct information on present-day English, or other historical records, and no information on other IE languages). Would these linguists reconstruct a single form, unspecified for number, for second person, while first and third person pronouns have distinct singular and plural forms? Irregularities in verbal and nominal inflection are at the present time steadily being eliminated (*dreamed* in place of *dreamt*, *oxes* rather than *oxen*); would any of these irregularities be retrievable? And what about the vocabulary superstratum of French origin (more than half on a dictionary count, but much less than half on a text count), which has different phonotactic structure from native Germanic vocabulary. These phonological differences might well become less evident as the language changes and the forms of words are simplified, eliminating many initial and final consonant clusters, etc. (something like what happened in the development from Latin to Spanish). Could the two strata of vocabulary then be distinguished? Different strata seldom have been distinguished, to my knowledge, in any reconstruction of a proto-language (except for Indo-European).

Studies of the proto-language that can be reconstructed on the basis of modern Romance languages, and then comparing this result with Latin (Hall 1950, 1976, 1983), and similarly for modern Indo-Aryan languages and Sanskrit (Southworth 1958), are instructive (although one must bear in mind that Hall and Southworth were already familiar with Latin and Sanskrit respectively). They show that what can be reconstructed for proto-Romance and proto-Indo-Aryan did occur in Latin and in Sanskrit but that only a part of the original linguistic system could be retrieved. That is, the reconstruction is a partial approximation.

We will discuss the question of proto-language further in §7, in the light of the punctuated equilibrium model that will be described in §6.

4.3 Dating

As noted earlier, languages change at a variable rate, depending on a number of factors. These include the internal dynamics of the language (the potential for change within the linguistic system), the degree of contact with other languages (and the types of structure in those languages), and the attitude of speakers. We have just a few scenarios with lengthy historical records – involving Greek, Indo-Aryan, Hebrew and Egyptian – and these extend to 3,000 or at most 4,000 years, a small fraction of the 100,000 or so years that language is thought to have been around.

What has always filled me with wonder is the assurance with which many historical linguists assign a date to their reconstructed proto-language. (And these are, by and large, people who firmly reject the glib formulas of glottochronology.) We are told that proto-Indo-European was spoken about 6,000 years ago. What is known with a fair degree of certainty is the time between proto-Indo-Aryan and the modern Indo-Aryan languages – something of the order of 3,000 years. But how can anyone tell that the development from proto-Indo-European to proto-Indo-Aryan took another 3,000 years?

One of the clearest discussions of Indo-European origins and dating is given by Mallory (1989). He suggests that 'the proto-Indo-Europeans were a Late Neolithic or Encolithic society which began to diverge about 4,500 to 2,500 BC' (p. 127). This dating is based on reconstructed words to do with pottery, domesticated animals (sheep, cow and horse), and agriculture, and what is thought to be the antiquity of these traits. There is a tradition of relating proto-languages to what archaeologists recognise as distinctive innovations in material culture. For instance, the Kargan culture (named for its practice of burial in deep shafts within a barrow) has been linked with proto-Indo-European. But why should a particular proto-language be related to a particular material culture, and not to some other? The varying opinions expressed by archaeologists suggest that there is generally an element of arbitrariness involved.

Really, linguistic dating should be based on linguistic evidence. But languages are known to change at different rates. There is no way of knowing how long it took to go from the presumed homogeneity of proto-Indo-European to the linguistic diversity of proto-Indo-Iranian, proto-Celtic, proto-Germanic, etc. The changes could have been rapid (as on Woodlark Island) or slow. We simply don't know.

After the Indo-Europeanists have had their say, scholars working on other families present their dates. Linguistic divergences thought to be of about the same order of magnitude as IE are accorded about the same time depth; or a little less, for a little less divergence; and so on. For proto-Algonquian about 3,200–2,900 BP has been given as a tentative date (Siebert 1967). For proto-Uralic, 6,000–7,000 BP is a generally accepted date (Campbell, forthcoming-b).

We noted earlier that the split and divergence involved in the Indo-European family cannot be the norm; this is an unusual occurrence. The later part of this expansion – the last 3,000 years, for which we have some written records – may have been very much quicker, or even very much slower, than the earlier part. Why couldn't proto-Indo-European have been spoken about 10,500 years ago?[15] This would correlate with a major socio-economic development, the introduction of agriculture, which archaeologists date at about 10,500 BP for this part of the world (see Harris 1996). Why couldn't proto-Algonquian have been spoken about 6,000 or 7,000 years ago (this would be fully compatible with the accepted date of 12,000 BP for the entry of people into the Americas)? Surely, the only really honest answer to questions about dating a proto-language is 'We don't know.' Or, one might venture something like 'probably some time between 5,000 and perhaps 12,000 BP'.

While working on the languages of Australia, over the past 30 years, I have at times experimented with the hypothesis that the languages are related as one family and then looked for a family tree model (an alternative scenario is discussed below). The question that then presented itself was: what could have been the date of the proto-language? After careful consideration, it seemed that the only honest answer is: it could be anything – 4,000 years BP or 40,000 years BP are both perfectly possible (as is any date in between).

The received opinion of a date of around 6000 BP for proto-Indo-European – with dates for other proto-languages being cali-

---

[15] The physical anthropologist Krantz (1988) provides reasoned argumentation for such a date. A similar date is suggested by the archaeologist Renfrew (1987) in a work which has received wide publicity; the author has an agile mind but lacks an appropriate training in the methodology of historical linguistics for his work to constitute a linguistically significant contribution to the debate.

brated on this scale – is an ingrained one. I have found this a difficult
matter to get specialists to even discuss. Yet it does seem to be a
house of cards (reinforced, at one time, by the chimera of glottochronology). This is a question that demands careful re-exam-
ination, with a full range of possibilities being discussed and
compared.[16]

4.4 Subgrouping

Reconstructing the subgrouping within a family tree – the ways
in which the splits occurred – can be a much more difficult matter
than deciding, in the first place, that this group of languages is genetically related. It relies on evidence that is not always available: a
number of distinctive shared innovations in each of a set of languages
within a family points to their constituting a subgroup, with a
common ancestor part-way between the proto-language for the
entire family and these modern languages.[17]

For instance, Danish, Swedish, Norwegian, Icelandic, English,

---

[16] The question of the place where a putative proto-language is likely to have been
spoken (the proto-homeland) is an important one, which is not discussed here.
Arguments generally turn on where certain flora and fauna (whose names can be
reconstructed) can be found, and on postulated correlations with stages of
material culture in particular places. All these types of arguments relate to the
question of dating – a certain animal or plant may have had different geographical distributions at, say, 6000 BP and 10000 BP. A further criterion that is often
invoked is that the proto-homeland is likely to be where the greatest diversity of
modern languages from the family is found; this is something which demands
careful reconsideration.

[17] The best statements I know of the criteria for determining genetic relationship
and the criteria for establishing subgrouping are Greenberg's two essays (1957:
35–55) 'Genetic relationship among languages' and 'The problem of linguistic
subgroupings'. In Greenberg's African, Indo-Pacific and American work he used
his method of 'mass comparison' and stated that this was a preliminary step. As a
later step the comparative method should be applied, with the initial hypotheses
confirmed by reconstruction of a proto-language for every postulated genetic
grouping. Neither Greenberg nor anyone else has taken this later step, for the
majority of the groupings suggested. See comments under (a) of §4.1 above.

Dutch and German are established as the Germanic subgroup within the Indo-European family by virtue of certain changes that they have all undergone (these are then said to have taken place between proto-Indo-European and proto-Germanic). One of the best-known is the set of sound changes known as Grimm's Law. An aspirated voiced stop, such as *bh*, became the corresponding plain stop, *b* (compare Sanskrit *bhara:mi* 'I bear' with the English verb *bear*); an unaspirated voiced stop, such as *b*, became the corresponding voiceless stop, *p* (compare Greek *kannabis* with English *hemp*); and a voiceless stop, such as *p*, became the corresponding fricative, *f* (compare Latin *pater* with English *father*).

Any attempt at subgrouping must take full account of areal features. In particular, if all the members of a putative subgroup are in contiguity with one another, their shared innovations may have developed recently, in one language, and diffused into the others; they would not then be evidence for subgrouping. But it can be difficult to tell whether this has happened or not.

One way of deciding can be to look at neighbouring languages, from another family, and see if they also show the features. If so, they are probably an areal trait; if not, they may well be an indication of subgrouping.

South America provides an ideal laboratory since each major language family is scattered in geographically separate pockets, surrounded by languages from other families. A subgrouping has been suggested for the Arawak family, for instance, but in almost every case all the languages of a subgroup are in a single geographical block (see Aikhenvald, forthcoming). What is needed – and this is work which has still to be done – is to examine the features that characterise each putative subgroup and see which of them is also found in neighbouring non-Arawak languages. Once these are discounted, any remaining shared innovations (if there are any) can be assessed as evidence for subgrouping.[18]

[18] Where languages spread into places where they have no neighbours then subgrouping can be a more straightforward matter. For instance, the Polynesian sub-

The difficulties associated with subgrouping can be demonstrated through two examples. The first is schematic. Suppose that language X splits into A, B and C. Modern languages B and C are in a certain area, distant from A, and share certain features (say, noun classes and tones) that are not found in A but do occur in other languages of their area. There are at least two possibilities.

(a) X split into A and proto-BC. Proto-BC moved into another area and accepted the diffusional features of that area. Later, it split into B and C, with the new features being inherited by both modern languages.

(b) X split into A, B and C with no intermediate subgrouping. Then B and C moved into their present-day area and both adapted to this linguistic milieu by adopting the features that characterise it. Being closely related languages they would be likely to develop tones and noun classes, from their own internal resources, in similar ways (since these internal resources would be similar).

The two alternatives can be schematised:

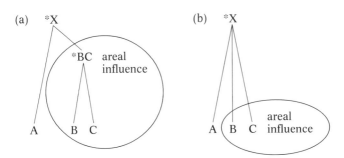

Figure 4.1

group spread out on the basis of one language per island with very little contact between populations and no borrowing. In this circumstance any development common to two languages is almost bound to be evidence of a shared period of linguistic development, i.e. of subgrouping. (There is just a slight possibility that each language underwent the same change after splitting had taken place.)

The point is that, given just the modern linguistic situation (with A, B and C), it would be difficult to distinguish between these two possibilities. We would not be justified in positing a subgroup consisting of B and C on the basis of shared features that also occur in neighbouring languages.

It will be seen that only a part of the subgrouping that has taken place in the development of a language family may be retrievable, just because of the limitations on the data that is available.

The second example is more concrete. Consider present-day German, English and French. Inspection of the modern languages shows that German and English are closely genetically related (sharing many grammatical forms and a high proportion of the most frequently used lexemes, including those with irregular inflections), but that English has a sizeable French superstratum in lexicon and to some extent in grammar and phonology. This is shown in figure 4.2.

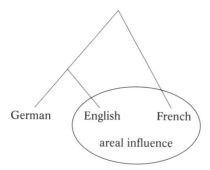

Figure 4.2

Now suppose that at some time in the future linguists only have data on languages descended from German, English and French (with no historical information). The grammar and lexicon of English will have undergone considerable changes in its descendants. Grammatical irregularities are likely to have been lost. Some Germanic affixes may have been lost and affixes of French origin may have become more productive (e.g. *re-*, as in *re-enter*, and *-ify*,

as in *glorify*, in addition to things like the already established *-able*).
In addition, words of Romance origin in English vocabulary could
be used more and more, at the expense of Germanic lexemes (this
already happens in Indian English – see Subrahmanian 1978; Kachru
1965, 1983; and Dixon 1991a).

If all these perfectly plausible changes were to take place, our
linguists of the hypothetical future might not be able to perceive a
close genetic link between reconstructed English and reconstructed
German. They could only posit the diagram in figure 4.3.

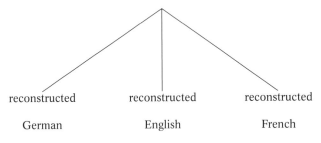

reconstructed   reconstructed   reconstructed

German   English   French

Figure 4.3

In summary, it is generally only possible to recover some of the
subgrouping within a language family. Lexicostatistics, of course,
provided a perfectly articulated family tree (with, as a rule, binary or
ternary splits); but this is based on vocabulary similarities, which are
not a sufficient criterion. The Indo-European situation makes the
point. Taking proto-Indo-European to be a single language, we need
a first split into no less than ten primary subgroups. Few of the people
applying an IE-type family tree model to other groups of languages
have been so forbearing – splits into two, three or four branches are
normally (though not invariably) posited.

❺ Modes of change

There are two basic possibilities – sudden or gradual – both for changes within languages and for changes to languages (language splitting). I discuss these in turn and then, in §5.3, consider the way in which language may have originated.

5.1 Changes within languages

I suggest that many types of change within a language are not gradual but rather happen fairly suddenly, often within the space of a generation or two. That is, change is more like a series of steps than it is like a steady incline.

If a new grammatical mechanism is innovated this is likely to happen all at once, rather than bit by bit. Bantu languages have about sixteen prefixes which combine marking of noun class and of number (singular or plural). It is unlikely that the ancestor language began with just one prefix, then added a second one a bit later, then another a bit later still, and so on, until eventually there were sixteen. I am not suggesting that this necessarily happened all at once (although it could have), but that there would not have been more than two or three stages involved. There might first have been a marking of 'human' versus 'non-human', for instance, and then more distinctions within 'non-human'.

When postpositions develop into a case system, the whole system is likely to evolve more or less at the same time, rather than one postposition becoming one case (an affix to a noun rather than a free form in syntactic construction with it), then a hundred years later a second postposition developing into a second case, and so on, so that a system of seven cases developed in seven separate stages.

Similarly with incorporation. When a language begins to place nouns within the structure of a verb (flanked on each side by grammatical affixes), this may begin with a couple of idiomatic combinations but will then, very quickly, be generalised to a fair-sized set of nouns (say, all major body parts, plus 'fire', 'water' and a few more nouns) rather than being gradually extended, adding more nouns a few at a time.

I am not suggesting that an established grammatical category cannot be added to. Once a language has a system of, say, five cases, others may well be added; or a new noun class; or further nouns may become open to incorporation. My point is that, when a new category develops, it will do so in a decisive manner. There will be no cases at all and then – within perhaps a couple of generations – a system of half-a-dozen or so cases, rather than one, then two, then three, . . . But then, as a further increment, a seventh case could well develop at some later stage.

Similar remarks apply to the development of bound pronouns. At one stage of a language's development subject and object are shown by free pronouns outside the verb. Then these develop into obligatory clitic pronouns that every verb must include (either for both core constituents, subject and object, or just for one). It is unlikely that the first person singular pronoun would first become an obligatory bound clitic, while other pronouns remained as free forms. In most cases (there are known exceptions, but these are rather rare), a fairly full set of bound pronouns would develop more or less simultaneously. (And then of course they may gradually become more integrated into the verbal word, with perhaps subject and object bound forms reducing and merging into a single portmanteau morpheme.)

When a language changes some part of its grammatical profile – say, from ergative to accusative or vice versa – this is also likely to take place fairly suddenly. In the north-west of Australia there is an

areal group of seven languages, the Ngayarda group.[1] Three of these
languages have an ergative system of inflection on nouns, like most
Australian languages – ergative case (-*ŋku* or -*lu* after a vowel and
-*tu* after a consonant) marks A (transitive subject) function while
absolutive (with zero realisation) marks S (intransitive subject) and
O (transitive object). There is also a case suffix -*ku* which marks the
peripheral relation dative. The other four languages have developed
an accusative system – A and S have zero marking with the original
dative suffix, -*ku*, being used for O (and also being retained for
dative). The mechanism of change is discussed by Dench (1982) and
Dixon (1994: 198ff.). The point to note is that each language from the
Ngayarda group has either a clearly ergative system of inflection in
its main clauses, or a clearly accusative system. There is nothing in
between. When the change from ergative to accusative happened,
it took place swiftly and cleanly.

Other examples of sudden changes could be added to those
given – the evolution of noun classes, of incorporation, of case
systems, of bound pronouns, and a shift from an ergative to an
accusative profile in some part of the grammar. I suggest that the
development of any grammatical category, or construction type, is
likely to be implemented by a series of step-like changes, rather than
gradually.

But, of course, some types of change are essentially gradual. The
great English vowel shift is thought to have begun by the
diphthongisation of high vowels ($i > a^i$ and $u > a^u$), with other vowels
then assuming higher places of articulation to fill in the gaps, as it
were. The whole process may have taken at least a couple of centuries.

And while the evolution of categories happens rather quickly,
their loss may be quite gradual. The loss of a category can be due to
phonological attrition, which is by its nature a gradual process. In

---

[1] Work is continuing on whether the Ngayarda languages should be regarded as
making up a genetic subgroup (Alan Dench, personal communication).

English, for instance, final nasals were lost and then final unstressed vowels; as a result of this, case endings disappeared (except for genitive -*s*). For example, there was a dative singular suffix -*e* (in the strong declension) or -*an* (in the weak declension) and also dative plural suffix -*um* (in both declensions); all these forms were lost, and the syntactic function that had been marked by the dative case suffix has now to be shown by a preposition, *to* or *for*.

We have said that when a new category is established in the grammar it may be augmented by new terms, which is a kind of gradual change. Overall, gradual change concerns matters of detail, while sudden changes relate to shift in grammatical profile.

Other gradual changes include: allophonic shifting within a phoneme (see, for example, Jakobson 1962: 202–20); the extension of meaning of a lexeme or of a construction type; analogising regular inflectional endings to replace irregular ones; the formation of new compounds (although the introduction of a new type of compounding is likely to be a sudden change); and the acceptance of loan words from neighbouring languages.

Some changes in grammatical profile are self-triggered, by the internal dynamics of the language. An example can be given from Australia. Originally, nouns inflected on an ergative, and pronouns on an accusative, pattern. Then bound pronouns developed, on an accusative pattern. Free pronouns were now used sparingly, mainly for emphasis. The internally motivated change was to inflect free pronouns on an ergative pattern, like nouns. (It could be said that they are now treated like a special kind of proper name.) This scenario has applied in Warlpiri, among other languages (see Dixon 1994: 96–7).

However, the majority of changes are due to the diffusion of a category from a nearby language or group of languages. If the languages with which speakers of X are in contact all have a system of noun classes (or genders), then language X is likely to develop its own system – generally, not by borrowing forms from its neighbours but by evolving noun class affixes from its internal resources (often, from generic nouns). And, as already mentioned, the process is likely to be completed within just a few generations.[2]

5.2 Language splitting

Every language and every dialect within a language is always in a process of change. The relationship between two adjoining dialects, or two contiguous languages, is never static – they may be moving closer together in some features and further apart in other ways. Neighbouring dialects or languages may gradually converge for a period, and then change direction and begin to diverge. This will be motivated largely by the type of contact between their speakers – friendly or hostile, whether they trade with each other, marry into the other group, take part in sporting or musical carnivals, serve in the army of the other group, and so on.

Once a nation or tribe splits into two, each with its own political organisation, the two groups will seize on linguistic features as tokens of self-identification. A handful of lexemes and/or pronouns can be sufficient. The dialects of two new nations or tribes may well be fully intelligible, the important political thing being to take care to use certain words and to avoid others.

Eventually, two dialects may diverge to such an extent that they cease to be intelligible and must be considered distinct languages.

---

[2] This can also be illustrated from Australia. The Yanyula language is on the edge of a region whose languages show prefixing and also noun classes, and both traits have diffused into Yanyula rather recently. There is a system of noun classes (or genders) shown by a prefix to the noun. One of these is the 'food' class, marked by a prefix *ma-*, which is plainly a grammaticisation of the noun *mayi* 'edible vegetable food' (this occurs very widely in Australia). Nouns in transitive subject function take an ergative case suffix. The interesting point is that when the 'food' prefix is added to a noun in ergative form, it has the form *muŋgu-* (from *ma-* plus ergative *-ŋgu*, with the first vowel assimilating to the second). Originally a transitive subject noun phrase would have consisted of generic noun *mayi* plus ergative case, and specific noun plus ergative case; it is the whole *mayi*-plus-case which has developed into a noun class prefix in this function (Kirton 1971).

This can happen in two ways, according to whether the dialects lose geographical connection, or retain it. We shall discuss these possibilities one at a time.

(a) *Language splitting under geographical separation*

Suppose that some of the speakers of a language travel to a new place (across the sea, or over the mountains) and live there, leaving the remainder of the speakers in the original location. Suppose further that there is no (or almost no) contact between the two groups. The dialects of each of the two groups will change, as dialects always do, and they will change in different ways – the dialects will gradually become more and more different. If contact were re-established after a period of X years, the dialects might still be mutually comprehensible. If contact were re-established after a much longer period, Z years, there would be no mutual intelligibility and we would have two distinct languages.

In this situation, of geographical separation, the development from one language into two would be a gradual process. This is because there is no contact between the groups; they are not trying to communicate with each other. Thus: [3]

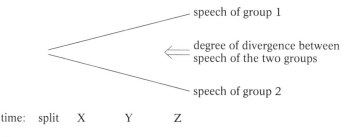

speech of group 1

degree of divergence between
speech of the two groups

speech of group 2

time: split   X   Y   Z

Figure 5.1

---

[3] Since languages change at different rates, it seems wisest not to suggest how many centuries might be appropriate for the points on this time axis.

Suppose that contact were re-established at an intermediate time. Some of the members of the first group, who had originally remained in their homeland, might now also emigrate to the same new land. This could happen at a stage (time Y on the diagram) when intelligibility is such that it is hard to tell whether we have two highly divergent dialects of a single language, or two distinct (but very similar) languages. If this happened the situation would quickly resolve itself. Either speakers of the two groups would establish close relations and each would accommodate[4] its speech towards that of the other group, establishing them as clear dialects of one language.[5] Or, in the other possible outcome, each group might adopt a stand-offish attitude towards the other, closing ranks and engineering further changes in their way of speech so that it became more different from that of the other group. Within a short time we would then have the clear situation of two distinct languages.

An example of splitting under geographical separation comes from Okinawa, just to the south of Japan. Sometime before 700 AD, Okinawa was settled by speakers of a dialect of Old Japanese. For the next 800 years or so there was minimal contact between Okinawa and Japan and, by the time of the first written records, at the end of the fifteenth century, Okinawan was mutually unintelligible with Japanese – a distinct (although closely related) language. Okinawa became part of Japan at the end of the nineteenth century and moved a little closer to Japanese (through loan words, etc.) while still remaining a separate language. The Second World War and its aftermath then produced a drastic change. From 1945 until 1972 Okinawa was administered by the USA and came into a great deal of contact

---

[4] An alternative is that a koiné could develop; this is a simplified dialect used for communication between speakers of two rather different dialects. Roughly, a koiné is likely to include features that occur in both dialects, but not those that are found in just one of them. (See the papers in Siegel 1993.)

[5] One of the dialects might be (or might become) socio-politically dominant, and there could then be unilateral accommodation, with speakers of the non-prestige dialect adopting some features from the prestige variety.

with speakers of Standard Japanese; Okinawans accommodated their speech towards Japanese. This has intensified since Okinawa was restored to Japan in 1972. Here the reunification happened slightly later than time Y in figure 5.1. Okinawan and Japanese had developed to be two languages; there has been a degree of creolisation involved in Okinawan changing to again become a dialect of Japanese. The younger generation can understand, but no longer speak, pre-1940 Okinawan, the form which is maintained by older people.[6]

Many language splits have involved geographical separation – much of the peopling of the Pacific Islands by speakers of Austronesian languages; the movement of speakers of Athapaskan languages down from Canada into New Mexico and Arizona; and, in all probability, the movement of speakers of what became Singhalese into Sri Lanka.

(b) Language splitting while maintaining geographical contiguity

We get a totally different scenario when two dialects develop into distinct languages and remain in contiguity, with members of the two groups still maintaining some degree of contact and communication. In this situation the split is rather sudden, thus:

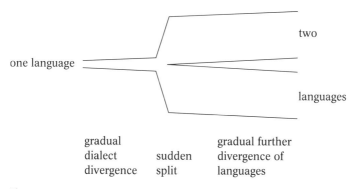

Figure 5.2

---

[6] Information on the Okinawan situation was provided by Masayuki Onishi.

I mentioned, in §2, that there is seldom much difficulty in deciding whether the speech of two groups constitutes dialects of one language or two distinct languages, when 'language' is defined in terms of mutual intelligibility. The intelligibility can be about 10% (two closely related languages) or 70% or more (dialects of one language); it is almost never around 50%. That is, once two dialects reach the stage of being different enough to lose mutual intelligibility and become separate languages, this happens rapidly, within a couple of generations. Each undergoes fairly radical changes in grammar and replaces lexemes at a faster rate than usual; there are also likely to be changes in pronunciation.

There is invariably political motivation for a split. Speakers of dialect A_1 develop closer social and trade contacts with their neighbours to the north, who speak a quite different language, B, than with speakers of A_2, a dialect of the same language, to the south. Similarly, speakers of A_2 will prefer to associate with and identify with speakers of a third language, C, to the south of them, rather than with speakers of A_1. A_1 will become more like B and A_2 will become more like C until A_1 and A_2 are two distinct (but closely related) languages.

In the 'geographically separate' situation, shown in figure 5.1, speakers of one dialect did not know of the existence of the other group, and how they spoke. Each dialect changed at a normal, gradual rate. In the 'geographically contiguous' situation (figure 5.2), each group is fully aware of the other, and the sudden escalation of diverging dialects into distinct languages is primarily a political move, to institutionalise political self-identity and demonstrate antipathy towards the other group.[7]

[7] One example of this involves Spanish and Portuguese. These could be regarded as divergent dialects of one language, or as two very closely related languages (see §2 above). Each nation tries to be as different as possible from the other – in language, and in other matters – to reinforce their separate political identities. For instance, in the orthography, different symbols are used for those sounds not covered by the letters of the Roman alphabet: Spanish uses 'll' and 'ñ' for the palatal lateral and nasal, while Portuguese employs 'lh' and 'nh'.

As was mentioned, if the 'geographically separate' situation were transformed into a 'contiguous' situation, at a time when intelligibility was at an intermediate stage, the situation would speedily resolve itself into 'one language' or 'two languages', according to the political and social attitudes between the groups.

5.3 The origin of language

If language split is typically sudden (save in the situation where two groups are geographically separate and unaware of the existence of each other), what then about the initial emergence of language?

There are two, polar, scenarios.

(a) Gradual development

An early group of people developed a very rudimentary type of language, with just a few words and maybe only one grammatical device – juxtaposing two words, an intransitive predicate and its argument (as when a young child's sentences are all of the form *mammy paint*, or *baby heavy*). A few more words and a little more grammatical complexity would be added every few hundred or few thousand years until a language with the complexity typical of modern language was eventually achieved. Under this view we would first get a rudimentary language (a few dozen words), then a primitive language (a few hundred words), then the post-primitive stage, followed by pre-modern and finally modern (many thousands of words and a grammar whose structures and rules need several hundred pages to describe in a reasonably full manner). If language development were gradual it could take tens of thousands of years to progress from the first linguistic awakening to the complexity of Swahili or Japanese or Finnish.

(b) Sudden development

At a certain stage of evolution people were able to think fairly clearly, although they had not yet developed a language. They had a well-developed set of mental concepts and could categorise things into classes, etc. Then language developed. Some words would have been onomatopoeic – the name for a bird could be based on its call, the verb for 'split' could be based on the sound of wood being split.[8] There would have been some sound-symbolic basis,[9] *oo* tending to relate to things that are large and round and *ee* to those that are small and thin.[10].

Language would have burst forth. Once there were names for some objects, names evolved for every type of thing and action and state and quality to which people needed to refer;[11] plus a full set of grammatical constructions to bind these words together; plus shifters such as pronouns ('I' and 'you'), deictics ('this', 'here') and time words ('tomorrow', 'today'). Once language developed, it would of course assist the process of thinking and concept formation, the two – language and thought – feeding each other and developing in tandem.

[8] Many modern languages have ideophones, sound-symbolic words that have grammatical function in a sentence. In a perceptive paper, Alpher (1994) describes a class of ideophones in Yir-Yoront, from North Queensland; it includes *thut* with the meaning 'assume a stable relative position' (presumably relating to the sound of putting something down). In Djaru, from Western Australia, there is a coverb *yut* 'sit' which, Alpher suggests, may have its origin in an ideophone similar to *thut* in Yir-Yoront.

Ideophones play an important role in many African languages, e.g. *pɛlɛ-pɛlɛ* 'small' and *wɔlɔ-wɔlɔ* 'forever' in Kpelle (Welmers 1973: 469). (And note English words such as *dilly-dally* and *wishy-washy*.)

[9] Sound symbolism (or phonaesthesia) is a topic scarcely mentioned in textbooks on linguistics. The trouble is that not enough is understood to say anything scientific about it. But it is too important a topic to ignore, and should be a high priority for future research. (Meanwhile, the interested reader is referred to Hinton, Nichols and Ohala 1994, and to the pioneering study in Reichard 1940.)

[10] *How* language developed is a large and difficult topic which falls outside the scope of this essay. Here I just offer hints concerning two of the many factors that may have been involved.

[11] Abstract terms naturally develop from concrete ones. In Xerente (Jê family, Brazil) the word for 'two', *ponkwane*, has an original meaning 'deer track', since the cloven deer hoof has two apposed parts (Rinaldo de Matos and Diana Green, personal communication); and in languages from many parts of the world 'five' comes from 'hand'.

I prefer the second alternative, of sudden development, as being more in keeping with the way we know languages change and split (once there is a language in the first place). This is, of course, a hypothesis that can never be incontrovertibly proved (any more than any of the hypotheses about the origin of the universe can be incontrovertibly proved). But it does explain a number of things. For instance, it is a fact that all the languages presently spoken in the world are about equal in complexity. There is nothing that could be called a 'primitive language' (with just a few hundred words and only a little grammar). When a pidgin (the rudimentary second language shared by two linguistic groups) develops into a creole (the first language of a group) within just a couple of generations it becomes a linguistic system comparable in complexity to any well-established language – in terms of size of vocabulary and richness of grammatical resources.

It may be that the reason there are no 'primitive languages' in the world today (or in recorded history) is that there never really were any. When language first developed, it was like an explosion. One would not of course have got to 5,000 words in one generation but I am suggesting that each generation would have added appreciably to the vocabulary they learnt from their parents. The human mind would have been mentally ready for language, and then it would have invented it, almost as a complete system.

There are further lines of support for this idea. We should first point out that there is no essential difference in social interaction between modern human societies that have varying economic bases. Contiguous ethnic groups in New York, or in the Saharan or Australian desert, or in the African or New Guinean or Amazonian jungle, all tend to have similar kinds of interaction with their neighbours, limited intermarriage, and so on. All of these situations involve complex languages – each consisting of thousands of words and subtle grammatical structures and constraints – languages which are difficult for an adult learner to achieve a full mastery of. Suppose there were primitive languages, each with just a couple of hundred words and minimal grammar. These would be easy to learn. Everyone would be able to speak everyone else's language. Unless there were exceptional social constraints on language use, the languages would tend to merge together, and with them the ethnic groups. The point being made is that the kind of social interaction we are familiar with demands non-primitive languages. This is consistent with the idea that there never have been such things as primitive languages, except as a local and transitory phenomenon.

The question about which I offer no opinion is whether language developed just once (monogenesis) or separately in two or more places (polygenesis). Either of these seems to be perfectly possible. There could have been two or more groups of early humans, at about the same stage of mental development, who were living in different places and began to use language independently of each other. Or it could have happened just once.

❻ The punctuated equilibrium model

The hypothesis put forward here to describe and explain the development of language during the 100,000 or more years since its first emergence is that there have been long periods of equilibrium during which a number of languages have coexisted – in a more or less harmonious way – within a given region without any major changes taking place. From time to time the state of equilibrium is punctuated by some cataclysmic event; this will engender sweeping changes in the linguistic situation and may trigger a multiple 'split and expansion' (which would be appropriately modelled by a family tree diagram). The punctuation may be due to some natural event (floods, drought, volcanic eruption), or to the emergence of an aggressive political or religious group, or to some striking technical innovation, or simply to entry into new and pristine territory. After the events which caused the punctuation have run their course, a new state of equilibrium will come into being.

I suggest that, over the history of human language, periods of punctuation have been relatively short in duration, by comparison with periods of equilibrium. The last major punctuation began in the fifteenth century, with European colonisation of almost all the rest of the world, and is still in mid-stream; this has led, or is leading, to the extinction of the great majority of languages.

European scientists have only ever been able to observe a time of punctuation since, wherever Europeans go (with their weapons and religions and writing), they effect a punctuation in the existing state of equilibrium. It is, in the nature of events, impossible for a linguist to observe a state of equilibrium since that very observation is bound to interrupt it. But the hypothesis of sustained periods of equilibrium is necessary to explain how language has developed, and to explain the present-day linguistic situations in many parts of the world. It is likely that Australia has had the longest period of equilibrium, without any serious punctuation. In this instance, the equilibrium state can be readily reconstructed; indeed – as I shall demonstrate below (and see Dixon, forthcoming) – it is the only model able to explain the relationships between languages in Australia.

§6.1 discusses the equilibrium situation and §6.2 deals with types of punctuation. Then, in §6.3, a number of particular geographical situations are considered.

6.1 Linguistic equilibrium

As a period of punctuation draws to a close, the languages in a given area will gradually settle down into an equilibrium pattern. The societies that speak them are likely to be characterised by the following features:[1]

(a) There will be a number of political groups, identifying as such (to themselves, and to other groups) through each having: (i) its own distinctive dialect or language; (ii) a group and/or dialect/language name;[2] (iii) its own set of traditions, beliefs and laws; (iv) its own kinship system, marriage laws, and so on.

---

[1] This is, to some extent, an idealisation. See, for instance, the essays in Barth (1969) for definitions of 'ethnic group' (all, however, referring to societies in punctuation mode) and difficulties associated with these. The characterisation given here is based on the past situation in Australia and past and present situations in Amazonia (from study of the literature and from my own field work).

[2] Each political group generally has a name for itself, and will also be named by its neighbours. These names may differ; for instance, we have *German* (in English), *allemand* (in French), and *Deutsch* (in German itself). Occasionally we find a group that has no name for itself; but its neighbours always have one. The small tribe I have been working amongst in Amazonia has no name for itself (when pressed on this point its members simply say that they are *ee jokana* 'we, the real people'). But the neighbouring Jamamadi tribe call them Amara; and the non-Indian Brazilians in the region call them Jarawara.

(b)   Each political group would have a population comparable to those of other groups in the area. That is, one group could be, say, four times as big as another, but not a hundred times as big. (The overall population of the complete area will remain approximately constant during the whole period of equilibrium.)

(c)   All groups would be roughly similar in terms of life-style and beliefs. That is, they would have a comparable level of sophistication in the tools and weapons they possess, the sorts of shelters they build, and the food resources they have available. They would have comparable types of (non-aggressive) religious beliefs.

(d)   No group would have substantially greater prestige than others, over any significantly large portion of the area. There could be minor prestige associated with one group for a short period (perhaps due to some song or ceremony they had innovated) but this might soon shift to another group. The prestige accorded one group would not be maintained long enough for it to spread widely, or for that group to establish a power of dominance over its neighbours.

(e)   Associated with this, no one language (or dialect of a language) would have any extended period of prestige.

I am not suggesting that, during a period of equilibrium, the political and linguistic situation in a given area would remain entirely static. There would always be changes taking place – a perpetual ebb and flow. At the beginning of an equilibrium period there might be, say, fifty languages spoken in a given area. Some thousands – or some tens of thousands – of years later there might still be about fifty languages there. But they would not be recognisable as the same languages. As noted before, a language is always changing, although the

Randy LaPolla reports (personal communication) that he is currently doing field work among a large language group straddling the China/Myanmar(Burma) border, which has no name for itself as a whole. The Chinese on one side refer to them as Dulong (which the group in China have recently adopted as their own official name) while the Burmese on the other side call them Nung or Hkanung (the people in Burma have recently invented the term Rawang to describe themselves).

rate at which it changes can vary. And there will have been some languages that ceased to be spoken (they might survive as a substratum within another language), while there would have been some modest instances of language split. The point being made is that changes during a period of equilibrium would be relatively minor, and of a quite different order from the changes during a period of punctuation, when large numbers of languages may cease to be spoken within a short time-span, and there can be multiple split and expansion of other languages.

During a period of equilibrium all sorts of cultural traits will diffuse within a given area. In particular, there will be diffusion of linguistic properties (as described in §3; and see Schmidt 1872). In this way the languages spoken in an area will, over a very long period, become more and more similar. Grammatical categories will diffuse and these typically spread over a considerable region. Lexemes will be borrowed and a given form may be found in a number of languages over a more restricted region. In §3.1 we noted Sapir's estimation that the borrowing of grammatical forms is so slow as to be hardly noticeable in the relatively small period of linguistic history that is open to inspection. However, we are here positing long time-spans – long enough for there to have been significant borrowing of grammatical affixes, pronouns, and the like.[3]

During a period of punctuation a given language (whose speakers have a particular material or ideological ascendancy, and the prestige that this brings) may undergo multiple splits, establishing a language family for which a tree diagram is an appropriate representation – a group of modern languages that have *diverged* from *a common proto-language.*

During a period of equilibrium, languages in contact will diffuse

---

[3] Note that sometimes one can tell that there has been borrowing, without being certain which language has borrowed from which. That is, we may have two languages, X and Y (which are not closely genetically related) sharing a grammatical feature, and it may be difficult or impossible to tell whether X borrowed it from Y, or vice versa.

features between each other, becoming more and more similar. These similarities will gradually *converge*, towards *a common prototype*. We can thus say that language families are rapidly made during a period of punctuation (which may be a few hundred or a few thousand years), and slowly blurred during the long period of equilibrium (which may extend for tens of millennia) that follows.

It is instructive to enquire what the possibilities are for two languages in contact over a very long period of time. Could they conceivably merge? I believe that the answer to this question is 'no' (with a qualification to be added soon). All our observation of normal linguistic development suggests that a language never has more than one parent (although it may have considerable substratum or superstratum from what could be called 'step-parents'). There is no reason to believe that this would not apply in all circumstances.

Suppose that – in the ebb and flow of movement in an equilibrium situation – two languages come into contact and they have rather few lexemes and grammatical forms in common, together with differences in grammatical organisation. Their grammatical profiles – categories and construction types – will gradually become more similar. The shared vocabulary will steadily rise until it reaches the equilibrium level of about 50% (see §3.2).[4] The stock of shared grammatical morphemes will also rise, but at a much slower rate. Suppose that the two groups now effect a political merger (the numbers in one, or both, groups may have dropped to a non-viable level, perhaps through disease or a massacre). The emerging group will naturally adopt just one language. In its grammatical forms and in most of its lexicon it will be identified with just one of the original languages, although a significant minority of words and a smaller number of grammatical forms may have come from the second language (constituting a substratum or superstratum). The new language

---

[4] This figure certainly applies in Australia (see §3.2), a long-standing equilibrium area which has only been punctuated within the last 200 years. More work is required to ascertain the extent to which it applies in other regions.

can be said to have come from a single parent, that from which it received most of its grammar and lexicon.

Now consider a slightly different scenario. We have two languages that are closely genetically related, with similar grammars and lexemes. They move apart and for a considerable time have contact with different sets of neighbours. Eventually, they move back into contact. Suppose that the percentage of cognate vocabulary has dropped markedly during their centuries or millennia of separation – to, say, 30%. There will be borrowing in both directions and the figure will rise, until it reaches the equilibrium level of about 50%. However, during the years of separation the percentage of grammatical forms shared by the two languages will not have dropped to anything like the same extent – suppose that about 80% of grammatical forms are still the same between the languages.

If there were now a merger of the political groups speaking the two languages, what would the single language of the new group be like? At the grammatical level it would be hard to distinguish it from a genuine merged language – 80% or more of the grammatical forms were held in common between the two original languages and these will go into the new language. The balance would be likely to come mostly from one of the original languages, but a few grammatical forms may come from the other language. It is in terms of lexicon that we should be able to assign parentage. About 50% of the lexicon comes from the common stock but the remaining 50% is likely to be taken mostly from just one original language (the language that supplied most of the balance of 20% of the grammatical forms).

There are some language situations in Australia which suggest an alternative ending to this scenario. Warlpiri, the Western Desert language, and other languages in a block right in the middle of the continent have a set of synonyms for many concepts. In the Western Desert language, all the speakers in a community will know *waru, warlu*,[5]

---

[5] Note that *waru* and *warlu* appear to be cognate; they must have come into this language through different genetic/diffusional routes.

karla and *kunjinkarrpa* as words for 'fire'; and *karli, yirrkili* and
walanu for 'boomerang', etc. (information from Hansen 1984).
Although everyone speaking the language is familiar with these synonyms, one local group will tend to use one of them more than the rest,
while another group will prefer another (partly as a mark of in-group
identity). When someone dies and a noun similar to their name is
tabooed, it will be replaced by one of the synonyms; but the original
lexeme is likely to return to use after a decent interval.

How could such a lexicon, with multiple synonymy, evolve?
One possibility is in the contact situation just described. If two languages have a very similar set of grammatical morphemes and about
50% vocabulary in common, they may well merge. The new language
will take over all the lexemes of both original languages, retaining
them as synonyms. In this rather special circumstance we could
indeed get a mixed language, with two parents (necessarily closely
related). It has simply combined almost all the forms from both
parents.

6.2 Punctuation

We now consider the punctuation of an equilibrium period. This
is often associated with population expansion, leading to the frag-
mentation of one political group into several new ones and a corresponding splitting of languages, so that there will be one for each
political group. During a period of punctuation new languages will
develop at a steady rate. As the period of punctuation comes to an
end, it can be modelled by a family tree diagram. As a new period of
equilibrium sets in, the original genetic relationships of the family
tree diagram will become progressively blurred, due to the diffusion
of linguistic features throughout the equilibrium period.

The first punctuation associated with language would have been
the emergence of language itself. I hypothesise that a group of early
humans had been living for some time in a state of equilibrium.
Without trying to speculate on how or why they came to evolve

language, it is clear that this evolution would have produced a drastic punctuation to the equilibrium in which they lived. I suggested in §5.3 that language probably developed rather rapidly – from nothing to a system comparable in richness and complexity to modern-day languages. (Not quite as complex, certainly, but perhaps half as complex; certainly not one-hundredth as complex.)

The evolution of language would have added new dimensions to the life of these early humans. They would have been more equipped to cooperate together in all aspects of life, and to plan joint activities. It is likely that the punctuation would not have just involved the evolution of language. This could have been the trigger for the development of a more sophisticated life-style, better food gathering and preparation, leading to population increase and expansion into new territories. The first language-speaking people could have rapidly split into two, as social groups diverged in habits and habitat. And then these might have split again. It is likely that the evolution of language was just the beginning of a period of punctuation that led to the expansion of peoples and split of languages, creating the first language family.

Once a certain geographical area was populated, with language-using people, a period of consolidation would have set in – an equilibrium period. From time to time there would be further punctuations, although these would be rather rare events between long periods of equilibrium.[6]

The punctuation of a state of linguistic equilibrium could come about for non-linguistic or linguistic reasons. Looking first at the possibility of a linguistic trigger, one language could have evolved (from within itself, like a sort of mutation) some novel types of

---

[6] A period of punctuation will necessarily begin abruptly. But at the end it will gradually fade into a new period of equilibrium. Within a period of equilibrium there could be minor punctuations, affecting just some communities and their languages (perhaps leading to a minor split, with a small family tree), but without enough strength to spread and punctuate the equilibrium state in the entire area. Obviously, the full ramifications of this hypothesis have still to be studied.

grammatical category or clausal construction that made it more effective for certain communicative purposes. These might have endowed it with special prestige or dominance. Or one language could have come into contact with another which had a markedly different structure, and borrowed certain grammatical features which – added to its previous grammatical inventory – again gave it a communicative advantage,[7] leading to special prestige and/or dominance. In either of these cases the better-equipped language could split and expand, pushing other languages into extinction. These are topics that should be considered and investigated; but in our present state of knowledge they are simply speculations.

It is likely that most examples of punctuation stem from non-linguistic factors.[8] There are here two major parameters to consider: (1) whether due to (a) natural causes, or (b) material innovations, or (c) development of aggressive tendencies in a people (the development of writing plays a major concomitant role in this type of scenario); and (2) geographical parameters, either (a) expansion into uninhabited territory, or (b) punctuation confined within a geographical area, or (c) expansion into previously occupied territory. These will now be discussed, one at a time.

---

[7] There is a mistaken belief among some linguists that 'all languages are equal'. While it is the case that all languages are roughly equal (that is, no language is six times as complex as any other, and there are no primitive languages), it is by no means the case that they are exactly equal. (Slobin, 1982, shows how speakers of different languages master comparable parts of their grammars at a quite different rate.) I have done field work on languages in Australia, Oceania and Amazonia and they were certainly not all equally difficult to describe. There is no doubt that one language may have greater overall grammatical complexity and/or a communicative advantage in a certain sphere, over another. But this is a topic for a separate book.

[8] There is a branch of mathematics called Catastrophe Theory, which deals with abrupt discontinuities within a natural progression, as a feature of the nature of the progression (there is an elementary introduction in Arnol'd 1992). This may well relate to the idea of punctuated equilibrium as applied to linguistics; it is a topic for further investigation. (See also note 1 to Chapter 1 above.)

(1) Causes

There are three major types of non-linguistic cause for the punctuation of an equilibrium state of human living and language.

(1a) NATURAL CAUSES The first type of natural cause concerns the environment – drought, floods, changing sea-levels, and volcanic eruptions. Volcanoes, drought or floods may radically change a living area, making it less habitable. Population size may reduce, with some political groups disappearing and others merging. Living conditions could deteriorate so radically that some (or all) of the people in a certain area may decide to move (across water or over mountains or desert) to seek a better place to live.

A major change would have been a fall or rise in sea-levels – establishing land bridges to previously inaccessible places, or else drastically reducing living space and perhaps cutting what was one continuous area into two or more separate regions.[9]

A different type of natural cause would be disease. If some new virus were introduced into an area, something to which the people had little immunity, it could cause a drastic drop in population. (And if this happened at the same time as – perhaps by reason of – an invasion, the depleted remnant would be able to put up much less of a fight than they might otherwise have done.)

There is also the possibility of genetic mutation. All sorts of mutations are possible; there could be one that would add some extra advantage in food-getting, or in some other aspect of living. The

[9] Until about 10,000 years ago, Tasmania was part of Australia; the sea-level then rose, cutting it off. There is no evidence of any contact between Tasmania and mainland Australia during the intervening period. The various cultural traits that have diffused across all or most of Australia are thus absent from Tasmania – these include axes, spear-throwers, boomerangs and the native dog (or dingo) (Mulvaney 1975: 161). Unfortunately, there was a propensity among the white invaders to shoot first and ask questions later. As a result, little was preserved of the Tasmanians' languages (just a few words, but almost no grammar), so that we can say nothing concerning how the languages were affected by this long period of isolation from the mainland.

population in which it developed could, as a result, start on a course of dominance and expansion.

(1b) MATERIAL INNOVATIONS New tools and weapons will give the people who possess them a significant advantage in the game of life. The new implements may just spread across an area – pestle and mortar for grinding, sieves, graters, all sorts of pottery for cooking and storage, blow guns, bows and arrows, axes, boomerangs. An alternative scenario is that a group who get a powerful weapon will use it to further their imperialistic ambitions. Guns provide the prime example. In every conflict between a group of people with guns and one without, the first group has eventually won. And in every case the language of the gun-toters flourishes while those of the gunless people sink away – gradually but inevitably – towards extinction.

Means of transportation is another important innovation. Land transport such as carts and beasts of burden. But, more important than this, water transport. This includes canoes and rafts for travel on inland rivers, and also sea-going craft. These first of all provide great assistance for fishing, and can significantly increase the food supply. And they can also facilitate exploration and immigration into new lands.

Perhaps the most important material innovation was the invention of agriculture. There is speculation about the reasons why a group of people would – after tens of millennia of just foraging – get the idea of clearing gardens, planting crops and weeding them. It would have happened at times and places where the soil, climatic conditions and available plants were especially favourable. Agriculture is said to have developed independently in several different places (the Near East, South China, Central America, highland South America and highland New Guinea). Bellwood (1996) has suggested that this innovation may in several instances have been the trigger for a large-scale punctuation, with split and expansion of the agricultural people and their languages. The domestication of animals (with the exception of the dog), where it occurred, often followed the development of agriculture and served as a reinforcement (assisting in planting and cartage, and adding to the meat supply).

(IC) DEVELOPMENT OF AGGRESSIVE TENDENCIES The necessary scenario for a period of equilibrium is a number of groups living in relative harmony with one another, each more or less respecting their neighbours and their neighbours' ideas and religion, and not trying to foist either themselves or their religion on others.[10] The political groups would have been fairly small in size (ranging from a few hundred to a few thousand) and fairly anarchic in organisation. We can imagine them as being rather like Australian tribes before the white invasion in 1788; or being like some tribes that survive today in the Amazon jungle. There would be no chief, just a number of elders. Decisions on what a village group or a kinship group should do would be reached by consensus, with some senior members of the group guiding the discussion.

This equilibrium is likely to be broken if a hierarchy emerges. A local chief – endowed with sufficient charisma and rhetoric – may aspire to more inclusive power. A greater and greater area, and a greater number of people, steadily fall under his command. Then an army is raised, expeditions made to conquer other peoples. The purpose is to add to the power and wealth of the original tribe or nation, and particularly of its leader. (I have in mind people like Genghis Khan, Attila the Hun, Alexander the Great and, of course, Hitler and Stalin.)

Or a new religion may evolve. The 'deity' will convey a message to his high priest – who will also be endowed with charisma and

---

[10] I am not trying to present an idyllic picture of the 'noble savage'. There would always be fear of some neighbours (and probably of evil spirits), some skirmishes and killings. But these would invariably be confined to a local level, partly because of the small size of political groups, and partly due to a tacit understanding not to go too far. Australian Aborigines, for instance, would settle disputes by organised inter-tribal fights, but these were generally terminated before anyone got killed (or else, as soon as one death took place).

rhetoric – that all peoples must be given the joyous message (even
if they don't want it). It may be spread by the sword (as happened
during the first centuries of the Moslem expansion) or more subtlely,
as has happened when – over the past few centuries – a swath of missionaries from many Christian sects has infiltrated the tribal societies
of every continent. Of course not all religions are aggressive (those
that were practised by the indigenous people of Australia, Oceania,
Africa, and most of those in the Americas were not) but those that
are brook no challenge. 'We have the message which we wish to
share with all peoples – nay, we insist on sharing it.'[11]

If one group gains particular importance – through innovations
such as new weapons or tools or agriculture, or through being the
ruling elite of a nation or the priestly class of a religion, or just
through weight of numbers – then its language will become the
prestige language of that area.

When one has the situation of a prestige language and a number
of non-prestige languages in a given area, there is typically one-way
bilingualism. Many speakers of the non-prestige languages will
acquire some competence in the prestige language (they will need to
do this, for things like trade and education) but speakers of the prestige language are unlikely to learn much of the non-prestige languages.[12] To take just one example, in Zimbabwe today the prestige
language is Shona (spoken by more than three-quarters of the
population); next in importance is Ndebele. Almost all speakers of

---

[11] The arrival of a new and aggressive religion may have profound linguistic effect.
Perhaps the most rapid series of changes that are known for any language are
those that applied to Old Irish between about 400 and 600 AD. The language
spoken at the end of this period would have been quite unintelligible to someone
from 200 years earlier. These changes relate to the introduction of Christianity
into Ireland; we assume that there was a breakdown of communication between
generations (or perhaps between classes) as younger people adopted the new
faith and older ones rejected it.

[12] Just a few members of the prestige group will learn something of the non-prestige
language, e.g. traders (although even here a pidgin may be in use) and interpret-
ers.

Ndebele know some Shona but few Shona have learnt Ndebele. And this selective bilingualism extends further down. Within Ndebele territory there is an enclave of Kalanga, a language with fewer speakers and lesser prestige. Most speakers of Kalanga have competence in Ndebele (and also, of course, in Shona), but relatively few Ndebele speakers can understand or use Kalanga. Such situations are found in every other part of the world. Speakers of minority languages in Indonesia will know some Bahasa Indonesian (they are taught it in schools, hear it on the radio) but very few people whose first language is Bahasa Indonesian will have learnt a local language. And similarly in North America, South America, Africa, India and Australia.

Sometimes we find that speakers of a non-prestige language (who also, necessarily, know something of the prestige language) will purposely speak to their children only in the prestige language, in order to assist them to move out of their non-prestige social group and get a better life-style. This is one of the ways in which a non-prestige language loses its speakers and dies.

There is another feature which – while not precisely a cause of punctuation – is a strong concomitant factor.

(1d) WRITING AND OTHER FORMS OF COMMUNICATION
Writing is without doubt one of the most important innovations of humankind – important in two entirely different ways. The first is generally beneficial – enabling any type of information, or any literary work, to be available to a huge range of users, and assisting people in communicating over a distance, planning complex manoeuvres such as conferences, commercial enterprises and wars. The second is selectively beneficial – the great majority of written documents are produced in the prestige language of a nation.[13]

---

[13] Generally this happens because it is too time-consuming and expensive to produce school textbooks or newspapers in languages with just a small number of speakers. But it can be by decree. The present military regime in Myanmar (Burma) does not allow anything to be published in a language other than English or Burmese unless it is fully translated into English or Burmese, for them

Speakers of non-prestige languages are swamped by school texts, newspapers and novels in the prestige language; this is an active factor in these languages being discarded by their speakers.

I have suggested that during most of the history of mankind people lived in self-contained political groups, without any hierarchy of leadership – small communities each maintaining a degree of harmony with its neighbours. These groups did not have writing. Writing was not developed during periods of equilibrium simply because it was not needed.

It was only when larger states evolved, with kings and lords and armies and organised martial campaigns; and when organised religion developed with sacred texts, set prayers and the like; and when extensive trade channels were developed – it was only then that writing became useful and desirable. The earliest written records in Hittite and Sumerian and Egyptian tend to be lists of produce, commodities, occupations, etc. Soon after came a record of the exploits of the king (Nissen, Damerow and Englund 1993).

Note that there is no necessary connection between literature and writing. All societies have (or had) rich repertoires of oral narrative, poetry and song. Each member of the community would be familiar with such work, which was handed down by word of mouth through the generations. Homer's epic poems, the Vedas of Ancient India and the books of the Old Testament were all preserved orally for several centuries before, with the advent of writing, they were committed to paper. People without writing have a well-developed memory and store in their mind enormous knowledge of skills and literature. Once they acquire literacy, memory is no longer valued or fully maintained. The new attitude is: 'it's all in a book, we can always look it up'. As Plato warned: 'this innovation [of letters] will produce forgetfulness in the mind of those who learn to use it,

to be able to check the content. This effectively stifles all publishing in the many minority languages, since their speakers don't have the resources or energy to meet this requirement (Randy LaPolla, personal communication).

because they will not exercise their memory' (Phaedrus 1275, put into the mouth of Socrates).[14]

Writing is associated with large, well-organised political and religious groups; it is a vital component in regulating and maintaining these groups. That is, it is an integral factor associated with the types of aggression that punctuate a state of equilibrium. During recent centuries, as a dominant civilisation has swept across a new area, the indigenous inhabitants have been exposed to written materials in English, Spanish, Portuguese, etc.[15] They may be taught to read and write their own languages but all who do so will also be able to read and write the language of the invader. And there will be many times more written material available in the prestige language than in their local tongues.

Other forms of communication follow. Radio, largely in the prestige language. And then television. Some attempt may be made to put out a few hours a week of radio programs in local languages. But where TV is available people prefer this over radio. And it is too expensive to make TV programs in a language that has only a few tens of thousands (or less) of speakers.

The swamping and eventual extinction of small local languages by national or regional languages – which are the medium for instruction in schools, and are used in papers and magazines, radio and TV – applies in every part of the world. In Siberia, Chukchee is

[14] Useful discussion of the disadvantages and advantages of writing will be found in Coomaraswamy (1949), Harrisson (1937), Archer (1943), Dixon (1980: 86ff.) and further references therein.

[15] Most of the indigenous languages that survive in Amazonia are spoken by groups which live well away from the main rivers. A notable exception is the Pirahã who still retain their own languages although they live close to the Madeira, the major southern tributary of the Amazon. The Pirahã maintain an inward-looking attitude, with little curiosity concerning what the European life-style in Brazil has to offer. In particular, they have stated that they do not wish to have their language written, saying: 'No, keep the alphabet for Portuguese, our language is not to be written down.' This attitude has undoubtedly assisted them to retain their language. (Information on Pirahã from Dan and Keren Everett, personal communication.)

disappearing under the weight of Russian; many local languages in Tanzania are failing before the encroachment of Swahili; and so on – these examples could be multiplied a hundred-fold.

(2) *Geographical parameters*

We can again review the possibilities, one at a time.

(2a) EXPANSION INTO UNINHABITED TERRITORY There can be a number of reasons why a group of people, living in an equilibrium area, move into some quite new area. It could be that, with changing sea-levels, a land bridge has just opened up. It could be that, for one of a number of reasons, the original territory is becoming a less attractive place in which to live. It could be that they have recently acquired sea-going craft and can make the required journey. In these instances, the act of moving provides the punctuation. Alternatively, the state of equilibrium could have been punctuated by something like the advent of agriculture. The established principle of zero population growth is abandoned, the population grows and the people seek new territory in which to expand and practise their agriculture.

In an equilibrium situation the population must remain roughly stable. But once new territory is opened up numbers will rapidly increase. Birdsell (1957) carried out a thorough study of the relevant literature and suggested that a population will roughly double each generation if unlimited food and land are available. He calculated that it might only have taken about 2,000 years after the first arrival of humans in Australia for the whole continent to be populated. The number of people in Australia would have grown from one or two boat-loads to perhaps 1 million within two millennia; it then stabilised at that figure during an equilibrium period of some tens of thousands of years.

With population expansion comes the split of political groups and thus of languages. Following the first occupation of a new territory we get new languages developing at a steady rate. By the time the territory is fully occupied, a well-articulated family tree will be an accurate model of the relationships between languages. This will then become blurred as the ensuing period of equilibrium advances.

§6.3 will consider three examples of expansion into new territory – Oceania; Australia and New Guinea; and the Americas.

(2b) PUNCTUATION CONFINED WITHIN A GEOGRAPHICAL AREA It is possible for the state of equilibrium in a geographical area to be punctuated by something that originated within the area, and whose effects are confined to the area.

A putative example here is the introduction of agriculture into lowland South America. Before this happened it is likely that the Amazonian forests were fully inhabited by tribes of hunters and gatherers speaking a range of languages belonging to a variety of language families. Agriculture was probably developed in one place by one tribe and may then have diffused into some neighbouring tribes. This punctuation set off a series of population expansions and language splits. Agricultural people, speaking languages belonging to a small number of language families (principally Arawak, Carib and Tupí), spread over a large part of Amazonia (and, in some places, beyond), displacing or assimilating tribes of hunters and gatherers. There are today a few enclaves of hunter–gatherer groups living between the agriculturists (notably the Makú, Mura-Pirahã, Nambikwara and Guahibo people); they are probably remnants of the original hunter–gatherer population.

(2c) EXPANSION INTO PREVIOUSLY OCCUPIED TERRITORY The state of equilibrium in a certain area may be punctuated by invasion. The invaders are likely to have some material advantage (e.g. agriculture, guns) and/or to be spurred on by some political ideal (or sense of supremacy) or religious fanaticism. They exercise dominance over the original population and their language becomes the prestige language. Where the invaded territory consists of many small groups, each with its own language (as in the Americas and Australia), or where the numbers of the invader greatly exceed those of the original inhabitants (as in New Zealand), all the original languages will decline and will in time be replaced by the prestige language.

Where the invaded territory does have well-developed political groups, languages with millions of speakers and perhaps also one or more highly developed religions (as in South Asia and Africa), then the indigenous languages will not decline in use. But the language of the invader still becomes the prestige language, and after the invader has been expelled will still maintain this status (especially in countries with a number of indigenous languages). Indeed, in India and Nigeria, Indian English and Nigerian English are the lingua francas, used for communication between people from different linguistic groups. If these large multi-language nations continue in their present form (rather than breaking up into smaller nations, one for each major language group), then the influence and use of the erstwhile invaders' languages is likely to continue gradually to increase. Especially when, as is the case with English, it is the major prestige language of the world.

Very occasionally, the invaders' language may fall into disuse, as happened with Norman French in England; even here, though, it has provided a very significant superstratum within Modern English. Note that the number of Normans was relatively small, and they came from a similar culture with no major material or religious differences from the English. And there was just one major language in England at that time, as against fifteen national languages in India and eight or more major languages in Nigeria.

6.3 Some examples

Europe, Asia and Africa are connected land masses in which humans have been living for hundreds of thousands, perhaps millions, of years. It is presumed that language would originally have developed in one of these continents.

Archaeologists have been able to date the arrival of mankind in other parts of the world. A bit less than 4,000 years ago for expansion into the islands of the Pacific; about 50–60,000 years for Australia/New Guinea (which was then one land mass); and at least

12,000 years (maybe 20,000 years) ago for the Americas (there is general agreement that this involved crossing from Siberia at the Bering Strait). We will now discuss these three expansions, in turn.

(a) *Austronesian*

The Austronesian language family is easily the biggest (fully justified) family in the world, with over 1,000 distinct languages. Scholars recognise four first-order subgroups, three situated in Taiwan (each consisting of a handful of languages) with the fourth involving more than 1,000 languages spread from Malagasy across to Easter Island. The proto-homeland is, reasonably, placed at Taiwan. The trigger for the expansion of Austronesian people is thought to have been the acquisition of agriculture (Bellwood 1991, 1996). With this new skill the Austronesians spread south-west to the Philippines, Borneo and Indonesia, and south-east to the coastal regions of New Guinea. All of these areas are known to have been previously inhabited.

Soon after 3,500 BP the Austronesians set out from the Bismarck Archipelago (north-east of New Guinea) and colonised the whole Pacific, taking with them crops and pigs. Every island, beyond the Solomons, is believed to have been uninhabited before the Austronesians arrived there. Archaeologists are able to give fairly firm dates for this progress – in Fiji and Tonga by 3,200 BP and, last of all, in New Zealand by 800–1,000 BP.

The Oceanic branch of Austronesian includes about 500 languages, all believed to be descended from a single ancestor, proto-Oceanic, spoken less than 4,000 years ago. This is a classic example of expansion and split for which the family tree model is eminently appropriate. Because of the rapidity of splits not all can be uncovered – for instance, the current family tree has about a dozen primary branches under proto-Oceanic. But lower down the family tree a lot of detail can be reconstructed, especially within the Polynesian subgroup, where there was sufficient gap between splits for significant innovations to have taken place, which came through into each daughter language. (See Pawley and Ross 1995, Pawley 1981.)

The Austronesian spread into Oceania is an example of a people with agriculture and good sailing craft (together with exceptional sailing skills) simply setting out to explore new lands. Once they arrived in a particular group of islands, and had fully populated it, long sea voyages were used more sparingly. For instance, once New Zealand was fully colonised there is no record of the Maoris there making trips back to the central Polynesian islands, from where they had come. A period of equilibrium was just beginning. (Only to be punctuated by the arrival of Europeans a few hundred years later.)

(b) Australia

Australia and New Guinea formed one continuous area between about 120,000 BP and the rise of sea level at about 10,000 BP. The earliest agreed archaeological dates for human occupation of Australia/New Guinea are roughly 50,000 BP. In fact the sea level was low on a number of occasions around 50,000 BP (Chappell, Omura, Esat *et al.* 1996). At that time there would have been a number of short sea voyages required to travel from the south-east Asian land mass (which then extended to Bali) to Australia/New Guinea. Birdsell (1977) investigated a number of alternative 'island hopping' routes. For instance, a route from Kalimantan via Sulawesi to New Guinea involved 10 water gaps, the largest of 93 km, while a route from Bali to the Kimberley coast of Western Australia involved 8 water gaps, one of 87 km, one of 29 km, one of 19 km, with the remainder each being less than 10 km (it could be that both routes were followed, by different groups). (Butlin 1989 discusses a similar scenario.) The journey from south-east Asia to Australia/New Guinea is of particular interest since it would involve the earliest dated sea voyaging (indeed, the earliest attested cooperative activity of humans). The boats used were likely to have been more substantial than any in use among Australians and Papuans at the time of European contact (excluding those of the Austronesian population of New Guinea, who arrived less than 4,000 years ago).[16]

---

[16] A few modern-day Papuan groups do have outrigger canoes; it is likely that these were fairly recently acquired from Austronesian neighbours (or traders).

Australia and New Guinea only became separated into two land masses about 10,000 years ago. One might thus expect there to be genetic connections between the languages spoken in these two modern islands. In fact none have been found.[17]

The *c.* 260 languages of Australia (at the time of the white invasion, in 1788) show many recurrent similarities, and have been said to comprise a single language family. In New Guinea there are *c.* 200 languages of the Austronesian family, along parts of the coast and offshore islands, which are acknowledged to have arrived recently. Leaving these aside there are *c.* 700 'Papuan' (the term simply means 'non-Austronesian') languages of New Guinea and nearby islands, which divide into *c.* 60 small families (see Foley 1986). As mentioned in §3, there are in New Guinea a number of areal features both across the whole island and in particular geographical areas. Not until these have been more thoroughly studied will it be possible to try to distinguish between areal and genetic similarities with a view to investigating high-level genetic links. Despite the amazing linguistic diversity in New Guinea (the greatest in the world, for such a land area), only a handful of good grammars are available while most of the comparative work that has been attempted is of mixed quality and unhelpful (much of it is based on lexicostatistical counting). Little more can be said about the linguistic situation in New Guinea in the present state of documentation.

We often find that a language family, or a group of families, is associated with a certain type of terrain. In South America, for instance, the Tupí, Carib and Arawak families were largely confined

[17] Foley (1986: 269–75) discusses this matter and presents fifteen highly speculative similarities between recurrent Australian forms and forms in the Eastern Highlands languages of New Guinea. Half of these are monosyllables (not the best indicators of cognation), five of them monosyllabic verb roots. Work on Australian languages since then has found several dozen recurrent disyllabic verb roots; no plausible cognates have been found with Papuan languages. Any serious hypothesis of genetic linkage would require systematic phonological and morphological correspondences – very much more than Foley has provided.

to the jungles and the Jê family to the grassy plains. There are additional differences between these groups – Tupí, Carib and Arawak use hammocks, make pottery and practise slash-and-burn agriculture, while the Jê tribes lacked all of these things. There are also typological relationships between Tupí, Arawak and Carib, which set them apart from Jê (see Dixon and Aikhenvald, forthcoming).

Australia/New Guinea divides into two geographical areas. There is mountainous territory, covered with rain forest, over a good deal of New Guinea, with a finger extending down the north-east coast of Australia. The remainder of Australia is fairly flat country, with sparse forest, grasslands or desert. We would expect different kinds of languages to be found in the two areas. On the South American model, we might expect more linguistic diversity in the forested regions than on the plains. As just described, this is what is found.

What might also be expected is to find languages of the New Guinea type (and perhaps genetic affiliation) in the strip of mountainous rainforest down the north-east coast of Australia. It is likely that this was the case at the time sea level rose to separate Australia from New Guinea, about 10,000 years ago. There is evidence for a different kind of people, the Negrito type, in the rainforest around Cairns (Tindale and Birdsell 1941). But during the intervening millennia this area has been infiltrated by people speaking languages of the normal Australian type (there is discussion of this in Dixon 1977: 15–16).

We can now focus on Australia. There are early archaeological dates from all parts of the continent. It is likely that the whole of Australia was populated within a few thousand years of the first colonisation, about 50,000 BP. Many scholars believe that all Australian languages belong to one linguistic family. Assuming this hypothesis there are two alternative scenarios:

(i) Proto-Australian, the putative ancestor of all the modern languages, was spoken by some of the first people in Australia, about 50,000 years ago.

(ii)   Modern Australian languages are descended from a proto-language that was spoken much more recently – say, 10,000 or 5,000 years ago.

Under hypothesis (ii), languages of the modern Australian family would have spread out over the whole continent, displacing languages that were already there. There are two difficulties with this idea. Firstly, we might expect to find pockets of the earlier languages (probably up in the hills or in the deserts); there are none. Or we might expect to find a non-Australian substratum in some languages; none is evident. Secondly, it is hard to conceive of how one language family (consisting of *c.* 260 languages) could replace another over a whole continent. In other parts of the world, language replacement is due to imperialism and conquest; but small groups of hunters and gatherers would be unlikely to pursue conquest over more than a limited local area. It could happen through some material innovation, but there is no evidence of any sufficiently significant technical advance. (Although agriculture was developed in the highlands of New Guinea, there was none in Australia.) That is, such expansion would require a drastic punctuation, and it is difficult to imagine what a suitable trigger for it could be.

We are left with scenario (i), which is by far the most probable. Proto-Australian, the putative ancestor, would have been spoken by a small political group, of at most a few thousand people. With the food resources of a continent before them the population would have increased, groups would have moved off into new territory and languages would have split. By the time the whole continent was populated – which may have only taken a couple of thousand years – the relationships between the languages could have been captured through a family tree, the model that is appropriate after an expansion-and-split scenario.

Then, once the continent was fully peopled, a state of equilibrium would have been established, and continued for the balance of the 50,000 years until it was abruptly punctuated by the English invasion. As described in §6.1, nothing is static during a period of equilibrium – there are continual ebbs and flows. And there is continuous diffusion of linguistic features. Whereas during a period of punctuation many new languages emerge, diverging from a proto-language, during a period of equilibrium languages borrow back and forth so that they tend to converge towards a common prototype.

Australia (as at 1788) provides a prototypical example of a long-term diffusion area. Almost every feature that can be mapped – phonological, morphological, syntactic – applies over all the languages[18] in a continuous area, its range of diffusion. There is one striking feature that is sometimes taken to divide the languages into two groups – in an area in the central north, languages have developed complex verb structures with prefixes that include bound pronouns referring to core arguments. But this prefixing area does not coincide with other diffusional areas. For instance, some languages have only a small number of inflecting verbal roots; other verbal concepts involve combination of a non-inflecting form with one of these inflecting roots. The area in which this is found partly overlaps the prefixing area but does not coincide with it – some prefixing languages lack this feature while some non-prefixing languages have it.

In the days of lexicostatistics it was suggested that there were 29 'phylic families' in Australia, all but two or three in the prefixing area. One large non-prefixing 'phylic family', called Pama-Nyungan, covers about 85% of the continent. In fact (contrary to what has sometimes been said) there is no clear linguistic boundary between Pama-Nyungan languages and the rest. Isoglosses can be drawn for many types of linguistic features but they seldom coincide. Each feature has its own area of application (and most of these areas

[18] The situation is in fact more complex than this. We often find the boundary of a diffusion area passing between the dialects of a language. To quote just one example, bound pronouns are found in only some dialects of the Bidjara language from south Queensland, those dialects which adjoin a diffusion area for bound pronouns.

include some prefixing and some non-prefixing languages, some non-Pama-Nyungan and some Pama-Nyungan languages).

It is possible to establish low-level subgroups in Australia – groups of from two to a dozen or so languages that appear to have a close genetic relationship. With two exceptions, all of these are geographically contiguous. No higher-level family tree can be justified, linking the low-level subgroups. (This lack of an articulated family tree is another piece of evidence against scenario (ii) above. If proto-Australian had been spoken only a few thousand years ago, the split and expansion would have happened rather recently, and a family tree model should be applicable.)

The low-level subgroups suggest the following scenario: (i) all parts of the continent were inhabited; (ii) water resources declined so that large inland tracts became uninhabitable, with the population contracting to the coast and major rivers; (iii) the inland areas again became inhabitable, and people moved into those parts nearest them.[19] Step (iii) would have triggered many minor punctuations, each of which accounts for one of the low-level subgroups.

We know of no significant immigrations into Australia between the time the first Aborigines arrived and the white invasion. All the conditions were right for a long state of linguistic equilibrium in this area. The modern linguistic picture is of overlapping diffusion zones, and languages having a similar typological profile over the whole continent (with areal variations). We have a situation of convergence. This may originally have begun with languages that had developed from a single proto-language, although this cannot be proved with certainty. It is not impossible that languages from several different families came into the Australian area and have merged their character through tens of millennia of equilibrium contact and diffusion.

---

[19] In fact, steps (ii) and (iii) could have happened several times during the 50,000 or so years that Aborigines have been in Australia. All that the evidence allows us to do is reconstruct the last contraction-and-expansion of population.

The languages of Australia share many recurrent features (see Chapter 3). There are also a number of typological parameters in terms of which the languages differ. In some cases one can observe a cyclical movement of change within a parameter. For example: (i) in one area, bound pronominal prefixes developed from free pronouns, then subject and object forms fused, and then some forms underwent phonological truncation such that the full set of semantic distinctions (person and number of subject and of object) were no longer made; to remedy this, additional bound pronouns developed again from free forms; (ii) many languages have shifted from a predominantly ergative to a predominantly accusative profile, and two of them have completed the circle, becoming ergative again; (iii) noun class prefixes have evolved in all the languages over a region in the north, and then they have been lost from some of these languages (on the edge of the region), because of diffusional pressure from neighbouring languages that lack noun classes.

Dixon (forthcoming) provides detailed illustration of these cyclic movements, and also a full discussion of the diffusional situation in Australia together with suggestions about the origin and direction of spread of diffused features.[20]

(c) The Americas

North, Central and South America present a striking contrast to Australia – they include several dozen language families (none with more than 50 members) and a fair number of isolates. Until recently, the accepted archaeological opinion was that the Americas were first populated about 12,000 years ago. There have been some suggestions of an earlier date (16,000 or even 20,000 years) but these figures are

---

[20] It was largely in order to adequately account for the linguistic situation in Australia that I had recourse to the idea of punctuated equilibrium as a model for language development. This essay is – among other things – a prolegomena to Dixon (forthcoming).

by no means generally agreed on.[21] It is generally accepted that the populating of the Americas involved movement from Asia, over what would then have been a land bridge at the Bering Strait. The diversity of families in the Americas strongly suggests that quite a number of separate groups (maybe a dozen or so) – speaking different languages – made the journey.

The fact that so many language families can still be recognised is compatible with a time depth of 12,000–20,000 years (as compared to about 50,000 years for Australia). In South America, especially, languages from one family tend to be scattered into many geographically distinct groups, separated from each other by languages from other families. It was mentioned above (§4.4) that in the Arawak family each geographical group has features in common with other languages from its region, through diffusion. There are a number of linguistic areas where languages from distinct families are all converging on a common structure and phonology.

Nichols (1990) has argued that 12,000 years, or even 20,000 years, is insufficient time to explain the linguistic diversity in the Americas; she suggests a necessary time depth of about 35,000 years. I take a viewpoint that is diametrically opposed. The fact that so many language families are recognisable indicates a relatively recent series of language splits, quite compatible with a 12,000–20,000-year period. Give the languages in the Americas another 20,000 years and the diffusional patterns that are now emerging would become far more pervasive.

Since there is more geographical diversity than in Australia, we would not expect the whole of North America or the whole of South America to become a single diffusion area in the same way as Australia, but we would expect a great deal of diffusion of linguistic features over a number of smaller areas.[22] I suggest that in 20,000

---

[21] Meltzer (1995) provides an informed survey of claims for dates earlier than about 12,000 BP. He mentions that of the fifty sites identified in 1964 as having an older date, only four made a 1976 version of that list and none made a 1988 list.

[22] Payne (1990) provides a useful survey of grammatical forms that appear to recur in South American languages.

more years there would be such convergence of the languages in an area, to a common prototype, that the genetic relationships which are clearly evident at present (Arawak, Carib, Tupí, etc.) would become blurred, and no longer discernible.

For the three areas just discussed – Oceania, Australia and the Americas – archaeological research provides a time-depth for their first human occupation. Africa presents a different picture – humans and pre-humans have been in Africa for millions of years and it is a likely place for language to have first evolved, 100,000 years or more in the past.

As mentioned in §3, the current linguistic situation in Sub-Saharan Africa appears to be characterised by a number of over-lapping diffusion areas. There undoubtedly are some genetic groups but many of them still have to be proved. The most urgent task is to distinguish between areal features (which have, illicitly, been taken as marks of genetic relationships) and real indicators of genetic affiliation.

It does seem, from the information available, as if the current linguistic situation over most of Africa is part-way between that in the Americas and that in Australia. There are probably more genetic groups recognisable than in Australia, but less than in the Americas; and there appear to be more widespread areal features than in the Americas, but less than in Australia. As stressed earlier, languages do change at different rates, depending on the types of political and social systems involved, the internal dynamics of the languages, the degree of contact with other languages and the structures of those languages, and speakers' attitudes. With this caveat, the general impression one gets is that the current language situation over most of Africa indicates a time-depth for the linguistic area somewhere between those of the Americas and of Australia.

In summary, two of the main points of the punctuated equilibrium model of language development are:

(a) During a period of punctuation one typically gets an expansion-and-split scenario, of peoples and of their languages. This is where a family tree model is appropriate – a number of separate languages diverge from a common proto-language.

(b) During the long periods of linguistic equilibrium that intervene between punctuations, the people in a given area live in relative harmony. Many cultural traits, including many linguistic traits, diffuse. The languages in the area will become more similar – they will converge towards a common prototype. In time, the convergence will obscure the original genetic relationships (the end points of the family trees during the last period of punctuation).

A key point is that language split is almost always accompanied by expansion into new territory. There is an apparent counter-example to this. The North-east Caucasian (Nakh-Daghestanian) family, with 25–30 members, is thought always to have been located in its present territory. But what we have here is rugged mountain terrain. It is likely that one political group split into several, and that this happened a number of times, with each group having only limited contact with its neighbours. This could probably only happen in mountainous country. (Compare the *c.* 60 non-Austronesian language families in New Guinea with the putative single family in Australia – with about the same time-depth – as an example of the different kinds of things that can happen in mountainous country, which is difficult of access, and flat country, with easy communication.)

➐ More on proto-languages

Thinking in terms of expansion and split, characterised by the family tree model, comparative linguists typically regard a proto-language as if it were the result of rapid splitting during a period of punctuation. But it is probably not. A period of punctuation typically interrupts a long interval of equilibrium and the beginning of a language family is likely to lie in the type of linguistic situation that is produced by convergence within a linguistic area. Indeed, a language family may not have its basis in just one language.

§4.2 had preliminary discussion of how the putative ancestor language of a family should be seen as similar to the languages that are around us in the world today – with suppletions, irregularities, substrata, etc. Having now introduced the punctuated equilibrium model, we can take this discussion one stage further.

During a period of equilibrium contiguous languages diffuse features – phonological structures and systems (together with their phonetic realisations), grammatical categories, lexemes and (at a slower rate) grammatical forms. In a given area we may have two or three languages that have converged together in structure and, to an appreciable extent, in forms. They will belong to a number of distinct – although closely allied – political groups. They will be separate languages in terms of the strict criterion of intelligibility, although many members of the language community are likely to be bilingual or trilingual.

Suppose that the political and linguistic equilibrium in such an area is punctuated by the arising of a charismatic military or religious leader, or by the development of agriculture, or for some other reason. This punctuation may give rise to expansion and split, the establishment of a language family. The point to be made is that the language family may have emanated not from a single language, but from a small areal group of distinct languages, with similar structures and forms.

Such a hypothesis concerning the origin of a language family – an idea that follows naturally from the hypothesis of punctuated equilibrium – bears investigation. A thorough and unprejudiced study of the idea – for acknowledged families such as Indo-European, Uralic, Austronesian, Algonquian, Athapaskan, Mayan, Arawak and Dravidian – may decide that in some cases the idea of a single proto-language is most appropriate, but that in other cases the idea of a family developing from a small linguistic area explains the facts best.[1]

Not uncommonly, when reconstructing the putative proto-language for a given language family, one comes up with more forms – to which a particular meaning or function is assigned – than any one language is likely to have. For instance, two forms for a certain person/number combination in pronouns, or for a certain demonstrative, or interrogative, or for certain body parts.[2] This might well

---

[1] Note Meillet's comments, in his study of Indo-European dialects (1967: 169; my italics): 'Another conclusion . . . is that even before the separation Indo-European was composed of idioms which were already highly differentiated, and that *we have no right to view Indo-European as a single language*. The characteristic features of each of the large groups (Slavic, Germanic, Baltic, etc.) mark, to a great extent, the continuation of phenomena that do not belong to Indo-European in general and yet do belong to the Indo-European period.' (See also Trubetzkoy 1939.)

   Note also that for Algonquian, Siebert (1967: 39) says 'there is no proof that proto-Algonquian was ever an absolutely uniform mode of speech'.

[2] Bloomfield (1933: 318) remarked: 'The comparative method can work only on the assumption of a uniform parent language, but the incommensurable forms (such as *[-mis] and *[-bhis] as instrumental plural case endings in Primitive Indo-European) show us that this assumption is not justified.' In order to accommodate the idea of a uniform proto-language, Indo-Europeanists spend a great deal of time trying to 'explain' pairs of forms of this nature, but without reaching any consensus.

be an indication that there was in fact a 'proto-linguistic-area' (involving more than one language) rather than a single proto-language.[3]

Returning to the question of dating a proto-language, from §4.3, it will now be seen that a small linguistic area, which was the point of origin for a language family, may have existed for some thousands of years. Splits would have begun within this area, with dialects starting to move apart, before the burst of punctuation released a phase of expansion and split. It follows from this that the idea of assigning an exact date to a proto-language (or proto-linguistic-area) could be both chimeral and misleading.

The languages in a linguistic area – from which a language family developed – may all have belonged to a single original family or they may have been from several genetic sources. Or, if the equilibrium area has been in existence for a long period, the original genetic features could have been so affected by diffusion that family membership ceases to be a useful concept.

When discussing equilibrium periods, in §6.1, we suggested that, although there would have been general harmony between the political groups and their languages, the situation would always be shifting – a degree of ebb and flow. There would be a certain amount of splitting (although nothing like so much as during a period of punctuation) and some merging of political groups. On the principle that each language has a single parent, the language of a new political group would be identifiable with the language of one of the constituent groups, although there would be likely to be a considerable substratum or superstratum from the language(s) of the other group(s).

These sorts of considerations could explain some of the points

---

[3] Trubetzkoy (1939) commented 'there is probably almost no single word that occurs in all Indo-European languages. It is in fact the most widespread words that present in the individual Indo-European languages such phonological irregularities that their original form can be reconstructed only by doing violence to the facts.' This suggests that a proto-linguistic-area, consisting of a number of languages with many features in common, might be worthy of consideration.

of resemblance between postulated proto-languages of modern families. Consider, for example, Indo-European and Uralic.[4] Suppose that each did come from a single proto-language. It could be that Indo-European was language A_1, from family A, with a substratum from language B_2 of family B, while proto-Uralic was language B_1 with a substratum from A_2, another language of family A. Or these families could have originated in distinct linguistic areas, but with a language in one of the areas showing close similarities to one from the other area. There are similarities between Indo-European and Uralic languages (see, for instance, Campbell 1990) but they are explainable in a number of ways other than by positing a further, higher-level, family tree.[5]

A further alternative – and perhaps the most likely of all – is that Indo-European and Uralic had their origins in languages from different parts of the same linguistic area (perhaps a largish area, containing a few dozen languages) at the end of a long period of linguistic equilibrium. The two languages (or groups of languages) which founded the two language families, would have many typological similarities, and also a number of lexemes and a few grammatical forms in common. But it is likely that a close family-tree-type relationship between proto-Indo-European and proto-Uralic would not be demonstrable (as it is not for many modern Australian languages, despite their considerable structural and formal similarity). Languages in a linguistic area, at the end of a long equilibrium period, do show similarities, but these are an indication of convergence towards a common prototype, rather than being evidence of genetic affiliation. That is, we could get a situation like that shown (in a highly schematic fashion) in Figure 7.1.

[4] We could equally well have considered a different pair of families, e.g. Indo-European and Afroasiatic.

[5] Campbell (forthcoming-b) discusses loans from Indo-European languages into Uralic and finds none that relate to proto-Uralic. The oldest loans are from pre-Indo-Iranian and Indo-Iranian into Finno-Ugric.

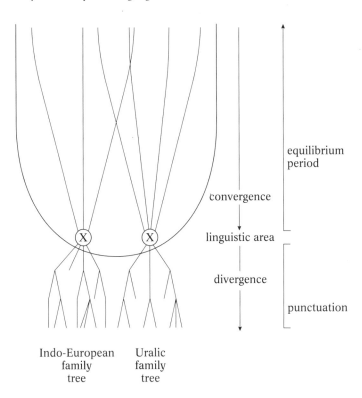

equilibrium
period

convergence

linguistic area

divergence

punctuation

Indo-European   Uralic
family   family
tree   tree

$\left(\text{X}\right)$ = one or more languages, as point of origin for each family

Figure 7.1

I began, in §1, by remarking that if the family tree is the only available model of linguistic relationship, people will try to apply it in all circumstances. If there are significant features in common between proto-Indo-European and proto-Uralic – ergo, they must be related in a family-tree-type way (the Nostratic fallacy). I have tried to put forward an alternative way of looking at things, an idea that was motivated partly by the need to describe and explain the modern linguistic situation in Australia, and partly to provide a hypothesis that will account for 100,000 years or more of linguistic development and interaction.

The relationship between Tibeto-Burman and Sinitic (Chinese) languages is a fascinating one that has not yet been fully explained. There are a number of critical lexemes that appear in both groups of languages, with regular sound correspondences. But it has proved difficult to progress much beyond this. (See, for instance, Norman 1988: 12–16.) If a number of wider models for relationship – going beyond simple family-tree splitting – were considered for Sino-Tibetan, one of them might provide a more appropriate scenario, and suggest further directions for investigation.[6]

[6] There is useful discussion in Hashimoto (1976a) where he suggests that 'it is still premature to talk about an established language family for Sino-Tibetan before solving the problem of cognate/loan distinction'. See also Ballard (1985) and Haudricourt (1961).

❽ Recent history

It will be useful (a) to summarise the way in which European dominance was imposed on most of the rest of the world, and then withdrawn; and (b) to outline the recent developments in communication; before (c) describing the ways in which languages and dialects have been and are being lost, and the reasons for this.

(a) *Invasions*

The white race originally lived just in Europe and the immediately adjacent parts of Africa and Asia. Then, from the fifteenth century, they began to colonise the rest of the world, establishing political dominance and imposing their languages – English, Spanish, Portuguese, Arabic, Dutch, French, German and Italian – on the peoples they governed.

The first continents to be systematically taken over were the Americas from the sixteenth century. These were followed by Southern Africa, South Asia, Indonesia, Australia and New Zealand, the islands of the Pacific, New Guinea, most of South-east Asia and, finally, almost all the rest of Africa. By 1910 the only major countries that were not governed by white people were Liberia, Ethiopia, Thailand, China, Tibet, Japan and Korea. Then, from 1947, the pendulum swung back. The indigenous peoples either seized power for themselves or were hurriedly granted it by their erstwhile masters (only France and the USA have resolutely held onto some of their colonial territories).

After the Second World War, white dominance was broken in every part of the world where the indigenous people still comprised the majority of the population – every nation in Africa, Asia, New

Guinea and the Pacific Islands. However, in North America, South America, Australia and New Zealand, the white race had established a dominance of culture and of numbers – the indigenous populations have shrunk to a fraction of their former size (through a combination of disease and murder) and remain an under-privileged minority in the new European-style nations. Many of their languages are dead, others are dying, and almost all the rest are endangered.

The invasions, emanating from Europe, punctuated the states of linguistic equilibrium that were in existence in many parts of the world.

(b)   Developments in communication

The period since about 1830 has seen major innovations in communication. Both transport – trains, steamships, buses, cars and planes – and media – increased literacy, schooling, newspapers, radio and TV. This has led to greater centralisation – people from rural areas can more easily visit cities and often prefer to live in them; newspapers, radio and TV programs come from the major cities. All of this contributes to narrowing the dialectal spread of a language, and to reduction in use of the languages of minority groups.

Once schooling was introduced, instruction was generally through the prestige language of the nation, and invariably in the prestige dialect of that language. Children whose parents spoke Irish or Welsh or the Yorkshire dialect of English were schooled in the London dialect of English and punished for any deviation from this norm.[1]

This applies just about everywhere in the world. For instance, in 1985 I lived for some months in the Boumaa region of Fiji which has its own dialect, mutually intelligible with the standard dialect, Bau. All instruction at the local school is through the Bau dialect. At one

---

[1] The content of classes is also generally monocultural, teaching about the history, culture and values of the prestige group, and paying little or no attention to indigenous culture and customs.

time children were punished for using their own dialect on the school premises; this is, however, now tolerated. All church services are conducted in the Bau dialect (the Bible is translated into Bau). One day I was invited to say a prayer and did so in the Boumaa dialect. For this I received a reprimand – God, the Christian priests had said, only likes to be addressed in Bau. Unsurprisingly, the Boumaa dialect is gradually moving closer to Bau; a couple of generations ago they shared about 80% vocabulary but the figure is now around 90%.

Aboriginal children of the tribes speaking Dyirbal, in north-east Queensland, were only allowed to attend the local school from about 1950. From then until well into the 1960s they were forbidden to speak in their own native language in the school grounds (and would be caned if heard doing so). Today the atmosphere is more liberal but education is still entirely in English. And, of course, the media that Dyirbal people are exposed to is entirely English. In 1963, when I began fieldwork, everyone over about thirty-five had Dyirbal as their first language; everybody except for a couple of very old people also had some competence in English. There were then perhaps a hundred speakers of Dyirbal. Thirty years later only those over about sixty-five can speak the language – there are just half-a-dozen of them. Some of the younger people are proud of being able to under-stand the Dyirbal language, as spoken by the older people; but in a few years there will be no one left to understand.

Improved communication, all over the world, is leading to the loss of language and also a great diminution in dialect differentiation. In England, in Fiji, and in every other country, regional dialects are gradually moving towards the standard or prestige language variety. The development of new languages comes from diverging dialects. Not only are languages being lost in the modern world, but the chances of new languages being created (except through creolisa-tion) are reducing all the time.

If things had remained as they were in 1800, American English and Australian English would be steadily diverging from British English; in time, intelligibility would be lost and they would be considered separate languages. But the innovation of the steamship and then of the cinema, radio and TV has produced a quite different situation. At the present time the three dialects are converging. As people in these nations watch each other's movies and TV programs, they pick up speech habits from each other – words and idioms and grammatical constructions, and even some habits of pronunciation.[2]

The equilibrium situation, as described in §6.1, involved a number of political groups, each with its own language or dialect, existing in an egalitarian atmosphere. No one group established dominance over its neighbours and no one language or dialect acquired a prestige status (except in a transitory manner, and over a rather small region). In the present-day world we have large political groups (nations), each with a dominant racial and/or social group. The language or dialect of the dominant group is accorded prestige and is used in the majority of types of communication. (There are exceptions in the form of nations with more than one official language[3] – such as Switzerland and Paraguay – but they are rare.)

In summary, developments in communication have reinforced the effects of white invasions, in providing punctuation of the linguistic equilibrium areas which existed in the world until recently. Even in places where the invader has now been expelled (or left voluntarily), the disturbance engendered by Europeans continues and increases. Africa was divided into a number of states, not on ethnic or linguistic or religious lines, but simply as an artefact of European colonisation. Almost every modern African state is ethnically and linguistically diverse, which brings with it political tension and some-

---

[2] In fact, some ethnic groups do consciously try to make their dialect different from that of other groups. But such efforts are mostly in the area of pronunciation, perhaps the most salient aspect of language use. Without people realising it, the grammatical conventions and lexical resources of their dialects are steadily converging.

[3] Even in nations with more than one official language, there can be a strong preference for some topics to be dealt with in one language and other topics in the other, e.g. Spanish and Guaraní in Paraguay.

times massacres. There is continual development of communication in these nations. A small number of languages (sometimes just one) are the basis for writing, schooling, newspapers, radio, films and TV. As a result, the minority languages – those with a small number of speakers – are shrinking towards disuse.

(c) Language loss

We can distinguish a number of situations in which languages have been lost, during the punctuation of the past few centuries.

(i) POPULATION LOSS This can be by murder or by disease. There are instances of whole groups being exterminated by the invader. The entire Yeeman tribe, from around Taroom in south-east Queensland, Australia, was wiped out in a massacre by white settlers in 1857. (Not a word of its language was recorded, all we know is the name of the tribe.) This kind of genocide was repeated throughout Australia, South America and North America.

An alternative was to capture a people, enslave them, and literally work them to death. The first people Christopher Columbus encountered in the New World, when he set foot in the Bahamas in 1492, were the Taino (an Arawak group). Within twenty-five years the Spanish had carried off the entire population to slavery on the nearby island of Hispaniola, where they died out within a couple of generations. Hemming (1978) tells how the European settlers at the mouth of the Amazon would travel upriver, capture a tribe, bring them down to work on their plantations under harsh conditions, then when they died out (often, within about ten years), go upriver again to capture and enslave another tribe.

The white invaders brought with them diseases – measles and smallpox and the common cold – to which people in other continents had no immunity. About half the Aborigines in the vicinity of the first British settlement in Australia, at Sydney, died of smallpox in 1789 (within two years of the Europeans' arrival). It is likely that the epidemic spread across most or all of the continent; and it was followed by further epidemics. By the time the white invaders reached a

particular locality the population was greatly reduced and demoral-
ised by the white man's diseases, and put up less of a fight than they
might have otherwise.

The same happened in South America. Brazil was colonised
from 1500 but Europeans only penetrated the densest jungles of
Amazonia in the late nineteenth century. Their diseases preceded
them; the Indian population had fallen to a quarter or less of what it
had been in 1500. The process of population reduction, merging of
tribes, and loss of languages has been continuous. The ethnologist
Franz Caspar (1956: 221) lived for a while among the Tupari tribe and
was told by them that 'in the days of their grandfathers and great-
grandfathers several small tribes had merged. Of every man and
every woman Topto was able to say without hesitation of what
extraction they were. There was only one man left out of each of
the "Vaikorotá", "Aumeh" and "Mensiató" tribes. Five were real
"Tupari". All the rest . . . were "Vakarau" . . . Even the present language of the tribe, he said, was not the old Tupari, for the minorities
had adopted the language of the Vakarau. But people could still
recall how the various tribes had spoken and Topto told me a few
words of the real Tupari language.' That is, a number of tribal groups
had merged and adopted a single language for the new combined
group (probably with substrata from languages of the other original
groups).

The same story is repeated all over South America and in other
parts of the world. It will be appreciated that investigating the language situation in Amazonia today is a difficult task. Many languages
have ceased to be spoken, through the merger of political groups, and
those languages that remain have considerable substrata from
varying sources.

(ii) FORCED LANGUAGE LOSS Sometimes a language has
died because the dominant group simply forbade it to be spoken, or
engineered things so that it could not be spoken. In Australia the sur-
vivors of a tribe (those remaining after disease and/or massacres)
would be split up by the authorities, with a few being sent to this

government settlement or mission and a few to that one. With scarcely anyone to speak to in their own language, they would naturally turn to English. A common practice at many missions was to take children from their parents at the age of seven or eight and place them in locked dormitories where they would be punished if heard to speak in the parents' language. This practice continued in South America, Australia and New Guinea (and probably elsewhere) until the middle of this century and was a major factor contributing to language death.

(iii) VOLUNTARY LANGUAGE SWITCHING In many situations a language is abandoned by choice of its speakers – either choice of parents, or choice of children.

As mentioned earlier, the speakers of a non-prestige language are likely always to know the prestige language. My first teacher of Dyirbal, Chloe Grant, was fluent in her own language and in English. But Chloe and her husband spoke only in English to their children, since they felt it would give them a better chance in the world. This undoubtedly did help the children, but the side effect was that they cannot now speak in their parents' language (and regret that they can't).

Irish is spoken today, as first language, by only a few thousand people in the far north-west of the island; they belong to the lowest socio-economic group. The middle class in Dublin is actively working to try to revive the language, but in many of the families in the north-west, parents are purposely speaking only in English to their children. As they remark, talking Irish while everyone else spoke English has left them as the most disadvantaged group and they see no reason to perpetuate this situation.

In other contexts it is the children who make the choice. They hear two languages spoken around them and opt for the lingua franca rather than their traditional language, for one or more reasons. They may themselves perceive that the lingua franca is more useful, that it is used by more people in more places. Or they may prefer the lingua franca simply because it is simpler in structure and

easier to learn. This is a major reason given by Yimas children in the
Sepik region of Papua New Guinea for speaking Tok Pisin, the
national creole, rather than confronting the grammatical complexities of Yimas. It is also the reason given by younger members of the
Paumarí community, on the Purús River in Brazil, for speaking the
local variety of Portuguese rather than Paumarí (which does have
a more intricate structure).

(iv) INVOLUNTARY LANGUAGE SWITCHING In an equilibrium situation, bilingualism would generally have been a two-way
process – many speakers of language X would also have competence
in Y, and many speakers of Y would know a good deal of X. Modern
societies are not egalitarian, and when one language has a prestige
status (through being spoken by the largest number of people, or
being used by the dominant group), bilingualism is likely to be one-
way.

If someone knows two languages they tend to use them in different circumstances. The local language will be employed in traditional
activities – ceremonies, hunting trips and the like – and the prestige
or contact language in wider circumstances – in the workplace, in
church, etc. The prestige language will also be employed, most or all
of the time, in school, in magazines and on TV. What can happen is
that the contexts in which the local language is used simply contract
and disappear. The language slips from use with the cultural milieu in
which it was the medium of communication.

This type of language loss has happened – or is happening –
with the languages of small minority groups (those with less than
10,000 speakers) in every country.

From about the late 1960s there has been a resurgence of pride
in ethnic identity – among Navajos in the USA, among Aborigines in
Australia, among Maoris in New Zealand, and so on. People have
reasserted a pride in their identity and in their language. But they
have also become aware that the language is gradually slipping from
use, that it is not being learnt by most children. Strenuous efforts
have been displayed to try to reverse this trend. In New Zealand, for

instance, there are now Maori-medium kindergartens, primary schools and high schools. However, this program is having only limited success; many Maori children are talking in a developing creole that mixes Maori with English.

A language is a difficult thing to learn, other than as a young child, and requires application and concentration. There has to be a utilitarian reason for learning it, something more (to judge from recent experience) than ethnic pride.

It is also the case that no language – once it has ceased to be used in everyday life – has ever been revived. Mention is sometimes made of Hebrew as a putative counterexample to this statement. But Hebrew was always in use, both as a written medium (in books, journals and correspondence) and in religious services.[4] It was augmented into the first language of a group – which did take unusual application and dedication – but this group had a political unity. Hebrew did not burst out as the minor language of a minority group, but as the official and prestige language of a nation. Only in these circumstances would such a resurgence be likely to happen.

There are many small ethnic groups in the more remote parts of the world whose languages appear, at the present time, not to be threatened. This is simply because they have as yet little communication with the outside world. During the past five years I have worked among the Jarawara people, in Southern Amazonia. There are about 150 of them, in 7 remote jungle villages, all with Jarawara as first language, but almost all with a rudimentary knowledge of Portuguese (for trading with nearby whites for clothing, ammunition, batteries, salt, sugar and the like). The Jarawara have justifiable aspirations to be accorded the same social benefits as other citizens of Brazil – a school,

---

[4] As Hebrew came to be adopted as the language of everyday conversation, by people whose native languages were of the Indo-European family (Yiddish, German, French, Russian, etc.), it took on some Indo-European features. For instance, interrogative pronouns are now used as introducers of relative clauses, something that was not found in earlier stages of Hebrew (Aya Katz and Alexandra Aikhenvald, personal communication).

a medical post, access to TV. When this happens it is bound to impinge upon the language. The population is small; if some Jarawara should prefer to move, and live in the nearest town, it will disrupt the community and threaten the language. If the world continues on its present course, it is just a matter of time before the Jarawara lose their traditional culture and language, as has happened in other parts of Brazil and other parts of the world. The only way for such a small group – in the Amazon, in New Guinea or in Africa – to maintain its own language is to remain in isolation from the rest of the world.

Something can be done. Writing can be put to good use in producing primers for use in local schools (although children will never speak a local language from just having it taught to them in school, if it is not also used in the home). And writing can also be used to record traditional stories and songs. The language can be documented, before it vanishes. The loss of a language can be slowed a little; but it cannot be halted or reversed.

It is appropriate to pay some attention to the effect of Christian missionaries since they have – for the past four or five centuries – played a major role in recording languages, often in hastening their demise, and more recently in attempting to assist their survival.

The early Catholic missionaries in the Americas often applied force (plus threats of eternal damnation) to get an indigenous group to abandon its culture, religion and language. More recently, evangelical and other (including some Catholic) groups have adopted a different stance. They wish to translate the New Testament into the local language so that the people may adopt Christianity in their own language. The sad part of it is that every one of these languages is diminishing in use or dying. It is not unknown for there to be no speakers left at all, by the time the translation is completed. To quote two Australian examples, Threlkeld (1857, published 1892: 126) introduced the publication of his Bible translation by lamenting that, during the 20 years he was working on Awabakal, the language had ceased to be used: 'under such circumstances, the translation of the

Gospel by St Luke can only be now a work of curiosity – a record of the language of a tribe that once existed'. And, 140 years later at the other end of the continent, Jean Kirton – after 30 years of studying the grammar of Yanyula and translating parts of the Bible – noted 'with deep personal sorrow' that the language was no longer being learnt by children (Kirton and Charlie 1996: x).

In almost every case I know of, by the time the New Testament had been translated into an indigenous language, those people who could read it were also able to read it in the lingua franca (English, Spanish, Portuguese, etc., or a creole). And this despite the fact that the missionaries had often tried to teach literacy in the local language but not in the lingua franca. Thus, Bible translation into small languages (with less than 10,000 or so speakers) does not make this material available to anyone who would not be able to read it anyway. Of course it does make it available in the local language, and some speakers may – for one or two generations – value this. But a concomitant effect is the attempt to replace the traditional religion – which is intimately connected with ethnic identity – by a general world religion. This tends to hasten assimilation into the world culture, which rapidly leads to movement away from the local language.

Missionaries tend – sometimes unwittingly – to introduce ideas from their own society which have a deleterious effect on the local situation.[5] One is the idea of a prestige language or dialect. There are

---

[5] An example will make this clear. In the early 1990s I observed an evangelical couple (an American missionary and his Portuguese wife) introduce UNO, a competitive game, into an Indian village in the Amazonian jungle. They taught the children to compete against each other, and to try to be better than each other, something that is entirely alien to their way of life. Then the missionaries brought another set of UNO as a present for the people. They had a competition to see who would get the game. These missionaries had no anthropological training and had no idea that they were introducing a quite new concept into the Indians' life (they might indeed have noticed that there are no words 'compete' or 'win' in the Indians' language). Unwittingly, the missionaries have imposed the values of a dominant group in punctuation mode on an egalitarian people who had been in equilibrium mode.

hundreds of local dialects in Fiji but the early missionaries decided to translate the Bible into just one dialect, Bau. It is true that Bau had a limited local prestige but the missionaries endowed it with more; this has been a major factor in gradually eroding the individual character-istics of other dialects, and causing them to converge towards Bau (as discussed under (b), earlier in this section). In the Vaupés River region of Brazil, Catholic missionaries found a multitude of lan-guages spoken. They chose Tucano, which had a limited local pres-tige, as the sole vehicle for their work. The result is that other languages of the region have died, or are close to death, as people switch their linguistic allegiance to Tucano. (In time, of course, Tucano will also fade, under pressure from Portuguese.)

Missionaries can have other effects, both good and bad. Their presence brings in the outside world, with a different set of cultural values. In many cases this contact had already been established; in the remainder it would have happened anyway. Missionaries with the appropriate sort of attitude can assist a tribal group to come to terms with the outside world that is stealing into their lives; they can protect them from exploitation and dispossession, and help by pro-viding medicines and an appropriate form of schooling. If the mis-sionary learns the local language it will assist the people to assert pride in their own identity. This may help slow the loss of language[6] (although, as stressed before, it can never halt or reverse it).

During recent years I have had the opportunity to observe, at close quarters, a number of evangelical missionaries in Brazil. There are some with a basic respect for traditional culture (including reli-gion[7]) who fill a useful role. But there are others of a different ilk, who do great cultural damage to indigenous communities. This type

---

[6] A specific example is quoted in Dixon (1991b: 246–7).

[7] For instance, in the early 1990s, a family of the Makú tribe had a sick baby. According to tribal culture, the baby would live if accorded ritual blessing by a specific shaman, but the family lacked the resources to pay the shaman. A Brazilian evangelical missionary, who was working with the tribe, paid for the shaman from his own pocket.

is intolerant of 'unbelievers' and forcibly suppresses the traditional religion in favour of Christianity, getting their 'Christian' message over essentially by a conspiracy of fear. Their aim is, basically, to convert the Indians into something like the missionaries' ideal of a middle-class suburban American community. I have also witnessed, in Australia, the later stages of such a campaign, where a people have lost their original identity but not acquired anything to take its place. They have lost their own culture and language, and all spirit.

Some missionaries do useful linguistic work, providing grammars and dictionaries. Indeed, well over half the material being published on dying and endangered languages is from missionary organisations; the quality of it varies from good to poor. (It is perhaps unsurprising that the most intolerant missionaries tend also to do the poorest linguistic work.)

❾ Today's priorities

The loss of diversity in the modern world is reaching critical proportions. The remaining forests contain plants with medicinal uses that are known to the people who live in the forests. In many cases their nature and value have not yet been investigated by modern medicine. How could they ever be, if the plants are destroyed as a consequence of forest-clearing, or if the people who know them are assimilated into the mainstream of their nation, thereby losing traditional knowledge?

Language is the most precious human resource. Each language has a different phonological, morphological, syntactic and semantic organisation from every other. Only by studying the varied possibilities across all languages can we gain a general picture of the nature of the human brain as it relates to language activity. By examining the ways meanings are organised in some little-known language, the linguist may shed light on some universal feature of semantic structure, or evolve some new mode of thinking that could help to deal with problems in the modern world.

The next section will provide examples of linguistic parameters, their interrelations and their sequential changes, illustrating why it is important to document every known language. §9.2 exposes a myth of modern linguistics that is crippling the discipline. And §9.3 details what the work priorities should be for people who call themselves linguists.

9.1 Why bother?

It is estimated that of the 5,000 or so languages spoken in the world today at least three-quarters (some people say 90% or more) will have ceased to be spoken by the year 2100, as a consequence of the punctuations engendered in the first place by European colonisation. It is an urgent task to document these languages before they disappear.

A typical hard-nosed response to this plea is: Why bother? These are insignificant languages spoken by insignificant peoples, odd tribes and minority groups that will disappear simply because of the relentless advancement of the great civilised nations of the world towards a global community. What interest can there be in the language of a group of hunters and gatherers who spend their days trudging over hot desert sand looking for lizards and grass seed, or of a group of slash-and-burn agriculturalists who move their village every few years because they've exhausted the food resources of that patch of forest? How can these languages tell us anything that we don't know already from studying the rich resources of French, German, Spanish, English and Russian, perhaps throwing in for good measure Finnish, Turkish, Hebrew, Arabic, Hindi, Japanese, Chinese and Swahili? It is the fittest who will survive. Let these meagre languages of primitive peoples pass into oblivion unimpeded. Maybe record a bit of a few of them, as a sample, but it is a waste of time and resources to attempt more.

This form of response reflects several illusions. The first is that people with a limited material culture must have a proportionately threadbare language. The reverse tends to be the case. Small political groups generally have an intricate social structure with an articulated system of classificatory relationships and communal obligations. (In contrast, the social networks of city dwellers are rudimentary, and could appropriately be described as primitive.) Associated with this social structure tend to go complex systems of pronouns, with several number distinctions (there may be separate pronouns for 'you (singular)', 'you two' and 'you all' and sometimes also 'you few'). There is often an inclusive/exclusive distinction for non-singular first person – this involves two different pronouns for 'we two', one referring to 'me and you' and the other to 'me and someone else, other than you'.

It is a finding of modern linguistics that all languages are roughly equal in terms of overall complexity. The areas of complexity vary between languages – one may have a simple verbal structure but complex nouns while another reverses this. We can only get an idea of the range of possibilities available to human languages by looking at every language individually and comparing their features in terms of a common theoretical framework. Suppose that a large meteor had fallen on southern Africa a few hundred years ago, wiping out all the inhabitants. Who would have imagined that clicks could be used as speech sounds? And if we were told that clicks could be used in words, who would have believed that one language could have fifty-five contrastive clicks, as are found in the !Xũ dialect of Bushman (Snyman 1970: 49–50)?

Certain grammatical categories are found in all languages, but they are realised in different ways. Take negation for instance. In European languages clausal negation is shown by a particle (like English *not*) which typically comes immediately before the verb. This is in fact the most common type of negative marking across the languages of the world. But it is not the only type. In quite a few languages negation is shown by an affix to the verb – a prefix or a suffix. In Kabardian, from the North-West Caucasian family, negation is shown by a suffix -*q'əm* to the verb in a finite clause but by a verbal prefix *mə*- in a non-finite clause (Kumakhov and Vamling 1995: 96). In a few languages negation can only be shown through a main verb which literally means 'it is not the case [that...]'. In Fijian the negative verb is *sega* and to express 'I didn't see you' one must use:

(1) *e   sega*   [*ni-u   rai-ci*   *i'o*]
     it   be not the case THAT-I   see-TRANSITIVISER   you

This is, literally, 'that I saw you is not the case' or 'it is not the case that I saw you'. (Fuller details are in Dixon 1988: 40, 279–84.)

It is a common belief that all languages have three tenses – past, present and future. This is far from being so. Biblical Hebrew, for instance, had no tenses, using instead grammatical marking for

aspect – perfective (an action with a temporal end, e.g. 'John sang a
hymn') or imperfective (an action with no temporal end specified,
e.g. 'John sang'). In Fijian there are past and future tense markers but
these are optional; there is no tense specification in sentence (1), for
instance. Snyman (1970) reports that the Bushman language !Xũ has
no grammatical marking for tense or aspect, although it does have
temporal adverbs such as 'now', 'long ago', 'yesterday', 'finally', 'then'
and 'will'.

In languages that do have a grammatical system of tenses, a
past/present/future distinction is rather rare; it is found in Classical
Greek but in few other languages. The most common tense system
has just two choices, past and non-past; this is found in Singhalese
and in Turkana, a Nilotic language from East Africa, for instance.
And there can be much more complex systems than are found in the
familiar languages of Europe. For instance, the language spoken on
the western islands of the Torres Strait, between Australia and New
Guinea, has no less than four past tenses ('last night', 'yesterday',
'near past' and 'remote past') and three futures ('immediate', 'near'
and 'remote future').

Negation and tense are familiar categories. We have been
talking about the different ways they can be realised, and the size of
the system. But there are some grammatical specifications that are
not found at all in the most widely spoken languages. One of these is
Evidentiality. It involves an obligatory specification of the type of evidence on which a statement is based, e.g. whether the speaker
observed it themself, or someone told them, or they inferred it, or
assumed it (or just had a 'gut feeling' that it must be what happened).
Evidentiality is found in languages from various parts of the world –
the Balkans, Tibeto-Burman languages, Classical Japanese (but it has
almost been lost from Modern Japanese), some languages from North
America and many from South America, both on the Andes and in
the Amazon basin (see the papers in Chafe and Nichols, 1986).

Some languages have just a two-term evidentiality contrast
(most commonly: eyewitness/non-eyewitness) but others make

additional distinctions. The most developed system is found in a
number of languages of the Tucanoan family and one language of the
Arawak family, spoken together in a small, tightly knit linguistic area
in the Vaupés River basin, overlapping Colombia and Brazil – see
§3.2. Here there is a system of five evidentiality choices (see, for
instance, Barnes 1984). Suppose that I want to say 'The dog ate the
fish.' I must include one of the following evidentiality markers:

(a) Visual – would be used if I saw the dog eat the fish.
(b) Non-visual – would be used if I heard the dog in the kitchen
(but did not see it) or if, say, I smelled fish on the dog's breath.
(c) Apparent – could be used if there are fish bones spread on
the floor around the dog, which looks satisfied, as if after a good
meal.
(d) Reported – someone told me that the dog ate the fish.
(e) Assumed – the fish was raw and people do not eat raw fish
so it must have been the dog that took it.

Wouldn't it be wonderful if there was obligatory specification of
evidence in English? Think how much easier the job of a policeman
would be. And how it would make politicians be more honest about
the state of the national budget. However, detailed systems of evidentials tend to be found only among non-industrialised people. Why?
This is a topic at present little understood, but it must surely relate to
the people's attitude towards specificity in talking, towards how
generous one should be in the communication of information, and
towards telling the truth.

A recent study of evidentiality in Amazonia has two main findings. (a) That a grammatical category of evidentiality must have
developed, independently, in at least six different places and times. It
appears that the cultural orientation of people in the Amazon basin is
such that they tend to evolve 'nature of evidence' as an obligatory
grammatical system. (b) That once a language develops an evidentiality system, this tends to diffuse into neighbouring languages. The
next-door languages take over the category – the idea of evidentiality

– but develop the actual grammatical marking of evidentiality
choices from their internal resources. (See Aikhenvald and Dixon,
forthcoming.)

There is a lesson to be learnt from this. If linguists hadn't gone
out into the Amazonian jungle – after having inoculations against
yellow fever, typhoid, tetanus and all the varieties of hepatitis;
loading up with malaria pills; and so on – to study these languages,
we wouldn't have full awareness of an important dimension of
human language, complex systems of evidentials.

As a final illustration of the variety across human language,
correlations between categories, and linked changes, we will briefly
look at two parameters: (1) different ways of marking subject and
object functions; and (2) different kinds of adjective classes.

(1) *Marking syntactic function*

The major clause type in every language centres on a verb, as
head of the clause. The verb requires a number of core arguments
(subject and object) which depend on the verb. A requirement on any
grammar is to distinguish between subject and object, so that one can
tell who is doing something to whom. Simplifying a little, there are
three basic ways of achieving this.

(a) BY THE ORDER OF ELEMENTS Thus in English the
subject precedes the verb and the object follows; by this means,
Fred hit Bill is distinguished from *Bill hit Fred.*

(b) BY MARKING ON THE DEPENDENTS[1] In many lan-
guages a suffix is added to each argument of the verb, indicating its
syntactic function. In Latin, for instance, a singular subject is marked
by -*us* and a singular object by -*um* with nouns from one declension.
Thus *Domin-us serv-um audit* ('master-SUBJECT slave-OBJECT hears')
is 'The master hears the slave' and *Serv-us domin-um audit* is 'The
slave hears the master.' The words in these sentences can occur in

---

[1] The terms 'head marking' and 'dependent marking' were introduced in a classic
paper by Nichols (1986).

any order, without change of meaning, since what is subject and what is object are shown by endings on the nouns.[2]

(c) BY MARKING ON THE HEAD The third way of marking syntactic function is found in languages where the verb has obligatory prefixes and/or suffixes providing information about the person and number (and often gender as well) of subject and object. Here the verb, with its pronominal affixes, can make up a complete sentence. For example, in Kabardian one can say *s-a-leɣʲas'* 'they saw me', where the prefix *s-* indicates 'me' as object and the following *-a-* is 'they' as subject (Kumakhov and Vamling 1995: 96).[3]

Let us now look at how a language can switch from one type of marking to another; here we will focus on types (b) and (c). Almost all linguistic change is cyclic, and a language can readily switch from head marking to dependent marking, and then back again.

(i) FROM HEAD MARKING TO DEPENDENT MARKING
Proto-Arawak, the ancestor language of the most extensive family in South America, is reconstructed to have had just head marking. With a transitive verb, the subject (A) was marked by a prefix to the verb and the object (O) by a suffix.[4] All modern Arawak languages retain the subject prefix. About half keep the O suffix but the remainder

---

[2] There are two main kinds of dependent marking. In Latin the transitive subject (A) has the same marking as intransitive subject (S), nominative case; and transitive object (O) has a different marking, accusative case. The alternative system is where S and O are marked in the same way, by absolutive case, and A in a different way, by ergative case. (A full discussion is in Dixon 1994.)

[3] Many languages combine head and dependent marking. In Latin, for instance, there is full dependent marking and also partial head marking since the verb includes information about person and number of subject; *audit* is actually the third person singular present tense (active, indicative) form of 'hear'.

[4] Intransitive verbs have a 'split-S' system. For some verbs (mostly referring to volitional actions) the intransitive subject (S) is marked by the same prefix that shows A with a transitive verb, and with other verbs (mostly referring to non-volitional actions and states), S is marked by the same suffix that shows O with a transitive verb.

have lost it. Tariana is one of this group and it has gained some dependent marking, a suffix -*nuku* which can be added to a noun in any non-subject function. Tariana has undoubtedly developed dependent marking through diffusional pressure from the Tucanoan languages spoken in the same linguistic area, which all have dependent marking. The important point is that half the head marking (the object part) has been lost, and some dependent marking (on objects and other non-subject constituents) has been gained, effectively in compensation (Aikhenvald 1996).

(ii) FROM DEPENDENT MARKING TO HEAD MARKING It is clear that at an earlier stage Australian languages were entirely dependent marking, using case suffixes to indicate syntactic function. In one geographical area the languages have developed complex verb structures including prefixes; there are obligatory pronominal affixes to the verb, indicating the person and number of subject and object. In some of these languages, gender is also marked by verbal affixes, at least for third person. It is just the general feature of head marking that has diffused across all the languages of the region – each language has developed bound pronominal affixes independently, from its own free pronouns. In all the languages (a) 'I saw him' and (b) 'He saw me' can be expressed as a one-word sentence, but there are different rules for ordering the components of the verb. Using A for subject prefix and O for object prefix or suffix, there are the following main possibilities:

- A-O-verb, i.e. (a) 'I-him-saw', (b) 'he-me-saw', e.g. in Djamindjung;
- O-A-verb, i.e. (a) 'him-I-saw', (b) 'me-he-saw', e.g. in Ungarinjin;
- A-verb-O, i.e. (a) 'I-saw-him', (b) 'he-saw-me', e.g. in Njigina;
- both A and O are prefixes to the verb root but the ordering depends not on syntactic function but on person: a first person marker precedes a second or third person form and second person precedes third person (whatever the syntactic functions

involved), i.e. (a) 'I-him-saw', (b) 'me-he-saw', e.g. in Mangarrayi.[5]

In languages with head marking (where this includes gender specification for third person), the pronominal affixes to the verb adequately indicate the syntactic function of arguments, so that dependent marking is no longer needed. An ergative suffix (marking a noun phrase in A function) occurs over most of Australia with the original form *-dju*. Some of the head-marking languages retain this (with assimilation and lenition giving *-dji* or *-yi*) but it is now used only optionally. Other head-marking languages have lost it, the shift to a fully head-marking system now being complete.

(2) *Adjective classes*

There are two kinds of adjective classes across the languages of the world. One is an open class with hundreds of members; new members can be added to the class, through borrowing from other languages or through coinages. The other is a small closed class. Some languages have only five adjectives, others may have a hundred, but in each case no new item can be added to the class. Languages with small adjective classes are found in every continent except Europe (see Dixon 1982), and they have similar semantic composition, typically including words referring to size, colour, age and value. Igbo, from West Africa, has just eight adjectives: 'large' and 'small'; 'black, dark' and 'white, light'; 'new' and 'old'; and 'good' and 'bad' (Welmers and Welmers 1969). It is relevant to ask what happens to other concepts that are coded as adjectives in languages such as English. Again, a general tendency can be noted – words referring to physical properties ('hot', 'wet', 'heavy') tend to be placed in the verb class (one says, literally, 'the stone heavies') while words referring to human propensities ('sad', 'rude', 'clever') tend to be nouns (literally, 'she has cleverness').

[5] If both A and O are third person, then O will precede A (Merlan 1982).

Large open adjective classes fall into four types: (a) adjectives are very similar in their grammatical properties to nouns – they show gender and number and case, like nouns (e.g. Latin and Spanish); (b) adjectives are grammatically very similar to verbs, e.g. they inflect for tense or aspect (as in Malay); (c) adjectives combine grammatical properties of nouns and of verbs (e.g. Berber languages from North Africa); (d) adjectives have grammatical properties which are distinct from those of nouns and of verbs (e.g. English). Types (c) and (d) are rather rare, most languages with large adjective classes being of types (a) and (b).

(3) *Correlation between head/dependent marking and adjective type*
There is a strong statistical correlation between the two parameters we have just outlined.
Correlations
(I) Head-marking languages tend to have an adjective class of type (b), where adjectives are grammatically similar to verbs.
(II) Dependent-marking languages tend to have an adjective class of type (a), where adjectives are grammatically similar to nouns.

The rationale is evident. Adjectives tend to be in the centre of things. Whichever of noun and verb bears the marking for syntactic function, that is likely to be the class to which the adjective class is grammatically most similar.

(4) *Consequential changes*
We have illustrated how a language with head marking may shift towards dependent marking, and vice versa. These changes tend to take place quite rapidly; they can readily be reconstructed. There is no doubt that a language can change from having an adjective class of type (a) to having one of type (b), and vice versa, but all the indications are that such a change would be much slower than one between head and dependent marking.

We can return to the Arawak and Australian examples of shift in the technique for marking syntactic function.

(i) FROM HEAD MARKING TO DEPENDENT MARKING
Proto-Arawak was entirely head marking. I described how Tariana has lost some head marking and gained some dependent marking. Proto-Arawak appears to have had an open adjective class of type (b), taking tense and aspect suffixes just like verbs. This is continued in the modern languages that retain full head marking. However, adjectives in Tariana – while still taking tense and aspect suffixes – have developed some properties that align them with nouns. Both adjectives and nouns can (in Tariana but not in other Arawak languages) occur with a classifier, e.g. the 'round thing' classifier *-da*, as in:

heku-da	'round tree (trunk)'
tree (noun)-CLASSIFIER	
matfia-da	'beautiful round thing'
beautiful (adjective)-CLASSIFIER	

In summary, Tariana has shifted from a head-marking to a mixed-head-and-dependent-marking profile and, in correlation with this, adjectives are moving from a pure type (b) system (like verbs) to a system with some features of type (a) (some properties like nouns).

(ii) FROM DEPENDENT MARKING TO HEAD MARKING I have said that at an earlier stage all Australian languages were dependent marking; many still are but an areal group in the north have shifted to be predominantly or entirely head marking. Australian languages have large adjective classes, invariably of type (a), being grammatically similar to nouns.[6] This is in keeping with our correlation.

Head marking has developed rather recently in the northern area. I have suggested that a shift in type of adjective class is likely to

---

[6] Indeed, for some languages linguists consider that a distinction between noun and adjective class cannot be made, e.g. Dench (1995: 51–55).

be a slower matter than a shift from dependent to head marking (or vice versa). In fact, there are just the first signs of a change in adjective type, in some of the head-marking languages. In Emmi, for instance, adjectives still take the same case affixes as nouns, but they behave like verbs with respect to negation. A noun is negated by the negative copula *piya*, but verb and adjective are negated by the particle *way* (Ford, forthcoming).

We can draw the following conclusions, following on from correlations (I) and (II):

(III) Languages change fairly easily from head marking to dependent marking, and vice versa.
(IV) If a head-marking language takes on features of dependent marking, its adjective class will tend to change – but much more slowly – to become grammatically more similar to the noun class.
(V) Similarly, if a dependent-marking language takes on head marking, its adjective class will slowly change to become grammatically more similar to the verb class.

There are other examples of these concomitant changes, but points (I)–(V) should for the time being be regarded as tentative, subject to revision as more languages are studied from this point of view.

These illustrations ought to suffice to answer the question 'why bother?' If one simply examines a few dozen languages, all spoken by large communities, nine-tenths of the diversity and complexity of human language will remain undiscovered.

Every language has it own genius, its own points of interest, certain things that can be said in it more clearly than in other languages. And only by describing every possible language – investigating the correlations between their categories, and the ways in which these change – can we hope to achieve a reasonable understanding of what human language is, how it can be structured, and the ways in which it evolves.

9.2 Some modern myths

There are two interwoven aspects to linguistics: theory and description. One must work in terms of a theoretical framework to describe a language – using theoretical notions such as phoneme, word, adjective, subject, object, relative clause, negation, tense and evidentiality. As described in the last section, descriptive work feeds back into theory, helping to refine and extend our characterisation of how languages vary and change, of what human language is like.

Modern linguistic theory originated from the work of the first grammarians of Greek, at about the time of Christ (and their work was founded in the philosophical ideas of Plato and Aristotle). Some hundreds of years earlier, the greatest grammarian of all, Pāṇini, wrote a grammar of Sanskrit. His work only became known in the West in the nineteenth century and was then assimilated into the Greek-based tradition. Over the past few hundred years work has been done on languages from every part of the world, with many aspects of linguistic theory being rethought, reformulated and refined as a result.

The term Basic Linguistic Theory has recently come into use for the fundamental theoretical concepts that underlie all work in language description and change, and the postulation of general properties of human languages.

If a linguist is properly trained, they must have a solid grounding in the criteria employed in Basic Theory, and also in descriptive techniques. In working out the grammar of a language, alternative analyses have to be posited, their advantages and disadvantages weighed, and a decision reached on which is the most appropriate. Consider the question 'What is a word?' There are two kinds of criteria – phonological (e.g. each word has one stressed syllable) and morphological (e.g. there is one inflectional affix per word). Sometimes these coincide but other times they do not, and the linguist then has to recognise two units, Phonological Word and Grammatical Word, where a grammatical word may consist of one or more than one phonological words (or vice versa). (There is an illustration of this, for Fijian, in Dixon 1988: 21–31.)

We can offer a short illustration of how competing analyses may be assessed, also from Fijian (Dixon 1988: 26). This language has two phonological constraints: (1) a monosyllabic word must include a long vowel or diphthong, not just a short vowel; (2) if a word has a final short vowel, the penultimate vowel must also be short, i.e. it cannot be long. Now consider the two words:[7]

> *caa* 'bad'   *ca-ta* 'consider bad, hate'

That is, we have a root *caa/ca*. Used without a suffix it is an adjective 'bad'; used with the transitive suffix *-ta* it is a transitive verb 'consider bad, hate'. The question is: what is the form of the underlying root, *caa* or *ca*? Either choice is plausible:

(a) One could take the underlying form to be *caa*, and specify that the vowel is shortened, giving *ca*, when the suffix *-ta* is added, to satisfy rule (2), that we cannot get a long vowel in the penultimate syllable of a word when the final vowel is short.
(b) Or one could take the underlying form to be *ca*, and say that the short vowel is lengthened when no suffix follows, to satisfy rule (1), that a monosyllabic word cannot contain just a short vowel.

How do we choose between these alternatives? The basis for choice comes from another part of the grammar. There is a process of partial reduplication which applies to just a handful of adjectives, with plural meaning. Consider:

> *levu* 'big'   *le-levu* 'lots of big things'
> *vou* 'new'   *vo-vou* 'lots of new things'
> *caa* 'bad'   *ca-caa* 'lots of bad things'

The process repeats, before the root, the initial consonant and following short vowel. Note that for *vou* it is just the *o*, not the whole *ou*, that is included in the reduplication.

---

[7] In the Fijian orthography, *c* represents a voiced apico-dental fricative (rather like the initial sound in English *this*).

Now consider alternative analyses (a) and (b):

(a) if the underlying form were *caa*, reduplication would yield *ca-caa*.

(b) if the underlying form were *ca*, reduplication would yield *ca-ca*, which would be a perfectly acceptable word in the language.

In fact the reduplicated form is *ca-caa*, indicating that (a) is the most appropriate analysis, with the underlying root being taken to be *caa*.

To become a professional in any field one has to undertake the appropriate training, and then serve an apprenticeship. A surgeon attends medical school and then does routine operations before going on to do innovative work in, say, heart transplantation or plastic surgery (or to write a book on the principles of surgery, or on new directions in surgery). A linguist must be taught the principles of Basic Linguistic Theory, and also receive instruction in how to describe languages (through Field Methods courses). The ideal plan is then to undertake original field work on a previously undescribed (or scarcely described) language, and write a comprehensive grammar of it as a Ph.D. dissertation. Every language poses some kind of theoretical challenge, and solving this is likely to lead to feedback into theory, helping to enlarge and refine it.

At a later stage a linguist who has a thorough grounding in a particular language family and/or linguistic area – with good knowledge of one, or preferably more than one, of its languages – can embark on a comparative study. They may attempt to reconstruct a proto-language, or study subgrouping, or investigate types of diffusion (or combine all of these).

This is what should happen. This is what used to happen. But it is not what happens today over most of the world.[8] Over the last forty

---

[8] Australia is, by and large, an exception. At the Australian National University, for instance, about 80% of the Ph.D. dissertations completed in the 1970s and

years or so the discipline of linguistics has been knocked off balance. I will try to explain how this came about.

The major development has been the invention of a number of restricted sets of formalisms, that have been called 'theories'. Each is based on some part of Basic Linguistic Theory. Each is useful for describing certain kinds of linguistic relationships, but it is put forward as if it were a complete theory of language. The word 'theory' is being used in a novel way.

These formalisms (non-basic theories) tend to last for only a short time; the typical half-life is six to ten years. But while a particular formalism is in vogue – rather like a fad in fashion – its adherents proclaim it to be the only viable model of how language works. It is said that one shouldn't mix theories (just like one shouldn't mix religions) but in fact each is founded on a different part of Basic Theory, and it can be profitable to use ideas from different formalisms in describing different parts of a language. Of course, some excellent ideas have been put forward by people working within the various formalisms, and these feed back into Basic Theory.

A minority of linguists have continued as before, writing grammars of languages in terms of Basic Theory, and naturally expanding and refining the theory. However, they didn't have a name for the theory they were using; for them, it was just writing grammars, as people have been doing for millennia.

The formalists *do* have names for their 'theories'.[9] And they

---

1980s were grammars of previously undescribed languages. Just a few linguistics departments in the USA encourage their students to write grammars of languages for a Ph.D. dissertation, notably the University of California at Santa Barbara and the University of Oregon.

[9] I won't attempt a full list, but some of the theories of the past forty years are: Transformational Grammar, Standard Theory, Extended Standard Theory, Revised Extended Standard Theory, Government and Binding Theory, Principles and Parameters Theory (all of these associated with Chomsky), Tagmemics, Scale-and-category Grammar, Systemic Grammar, Functional Grammar, Daughter Dependency Grammar, Stratificational Grammar, Generative Semantics, Relational Grammar, Arc-Pair Grammar, Lexical Functional

often say that the people writing grammars of languages (something that, with rare exceptions, they do not do themselves) are working without a theory. As if one could possibly undertake any linguistic analysis without a theoretical basis.

It is only within the last few years that the term Basic Linguistic Theory has come into use, to describe the fundamental theoretical apparatus that underlies all work in describing languages and formulating universals about the nature of human language.

Each of the formalisms (the non-basic theories) provides a set of postulates about the structure of language, a framework into which every language can – it is believed – be fitted. When writing a grammar in terms of Basic Linguistic Theory one takes nothing for granted. Each analytic decision has to be approached as an open question. Is it appropriate to recognise one unit 'word' or two (a 'phonological word' and also a 'grammatical word')? Is there a construction type that has the properties normally taken as defining a 'relative clause'? Is it valid, for this language, to recognise a category of 'verb phrase'? In contrast, each of the non-basic theories posits that certain categories are relevant for all languages – one has only to find them. For instance, the Government and Binding formalism specifies that all languages have 'verb phrases', so that all one has to do is discover what the verb phrase is in a given language (one doesn't have to provide any justification for recognising a category of verb phrase).

When working in terms of Basic Linguistic Theory, justification must be given for every piece of analysis, with a full train of argumentation. Working within a non-basic theory there is little scope for

Grammar, Generalised Phrase Structure Grammar, Head-driven Phrase Structure Grammar, Cognitive Grammar, Role and Reference Grammar. The non-linguist reader will surely concur with my cynical comment that if a discipline can spawn, reject and replace so many 'theories' (in most cases without bothering to actually write a grammar of a language in terms of the 'theory') then it could be said to be off balance.

argumentation[10] – it is just a matter of slipping bits of the language into pre-ordained pigeon holes (and if there is some bit for which no slot seems appropriate, then that is of little interest since it falls outside the scope of that particular theory). Needless to say, such an approach tends to make all languages seem rather similar, and ignores the really interesting features which do not conform to any expectations.

The term 'analysis' is used in two quite different ways by linguists. For people working directly in terms of Basic Linguistic Theory, the analysis of a language implies recognising the operative elements of meaning, their underlying forms, and their combination and coding to produce a stream of speech. Adherents of non-basic theories use the term 'analysis' in a totally different way, to describe fitting a language into their axiomatic framework.

In fact few formalists do attempt to write comprehensive grammars of languages (which is just as well, since no formalism is fully adequate for the task). They sometimes work on just a bit of a language; this is generally not a sensible thing to attempt since each part relates to the whole and can only be properly understood in the context of the whole. Most often they confine themselves to working on their native language. But some of them do, from time to time, consult the descriptive grammars written by real linguists (in terms of Basic Linguistic Theory) and attempt to reformulate parts of them within their formalism.

There is one major myth in modern linguistics which is responsible more than anything else for the discipline losing contact with its subject matter, the study of languages. It goes as follows. There are

---

[10] William McGregor's Ph.D. thesis (at the University of Sydney) was a grammar of Gooniyandi, an Australian language, cast in terms of Systemic Grammar (a non-basic theory); this basically consisted in recognising in this particular language the items specified by the formalism. When revising the thesis for publication, he did include justification for the categories and structures set up, commenting (McGregor 1990: v) 'particular emphasis has been placed on argumentation, a consideration which has been consistently ignored in systemic theorising'.

essentially two types of linguist. The descriptivists, who do field work and write grammars. And the 'theoreticians' (i.e. the formalists, people working on non-basic theories), who do not gather data themselves but rather interpret it, from the point of view of their chosen formalism. The myth is that the work done by the 'theoreticians' is more difficult, more important, more intellectual, altogether on a higher plane than the basic work undertaken by the descriptivists.

This is *wrong*, from every angle. First of all, every person who describes a language is also a theoretician; they have to be, to make any analytic decisions. Every point in a grammatical description is a theoretical statement, and must be justified by appropriate argumentation.

I've worked on several fronts. I've written comprehensive grammars of several languages (some of which have had a deep effect on linguistic theory, e.g. Dixon 1972) and I've also produced a theoretical survey of the grammatical parameter of ergativity across every type of language (Dixon 1994). Each presented great intellectual challenges. But there is no doubt whatsoever that undertaking the analysis of a previously undescribed language is the toughest task in linguistics. It is also the most exciting and the most satisfying of work.

It is hard to convey the sheer mental exhilaration of field work on a new language. First, one has to recognise the significant analytic problems. Then alternative solutions may tumble around in one's head all night. At the crack of dawn one writes them down, the pros and cons of each. During the day it is possible to assess the alternatives, by checking back through texts that have already been gathered and by asking carefully crafted questions of native speakers. One solution is seen to be clearly correct – it is simpler than the others, and has greater explanatory power. Then one realises that the solution to this problem sheds light on another knotty conundrum that has been causing worry for weeks. And so on.

Some linguistics departments put on a Field Methods course but have it taught by someone who has never carried out original field work on a language (they have no choice, since not a single person in the department has ever undertaken field work). Most of these 'linguists' belong to in-groups; they support one another, help each other attain tenure and promotion. They argue that to understand language one doesn't have to work on languages; it can all be achieved by introspective cognition. This is rather like a group of 'surgeons', none of whom has ever actually performed an operation, giving courses of lectures on the principles of surgery.

By and large, the malaise of formalisms has not spread into historical linguistics. It is generally recognised that before one can profitably work on comparing languages one must have a thorough knowledge of one language – or, preferably, more – of the family or area concerned.[11] The difficulty is that comparison requires high-quality grammars of languages, something to compare. And too few linguists devote themselves to this vital task. The malaise of general linguistics, leading to a lack of good descriptive grammars, cuts off the raw materials for comparative linguistics.

9.3 What every linguist should do

A language is the emblem of its speakers. Each language determines a unique way of viewing the world. It encapsulates the laws and traditions and beliefs of its ethnic group. Indeed, a recent report on endangered languages in the USA (co-authored by a speaker of one of these languages) states: 'Each language still spoken is fundamental to the personal, social and – a key term in the discourse of indigenous peoples – spiritual identity of its speakers. They know that without these languages they would be less than they are, and

---

[11] Only in Moscow (to my knowledge) has the peculiar belief emerged that there may be such a thing as a 'trained comparativist', someone who can be let loose on a language family (without having done detailed work on any of the languages of the family, or having a close knowledge of any of them) and will then reconstruct the proto-language. These 'trained comparativists' have been 'trained' by aficionados of the Nostratic school (see §4.1). No more need be said.

they are engaged in the most urgent struggles to protect their linguistic heritage' (Zepeda and Hill 1991: 135).

Linguists can assist in this task. Documenting languages is the responsibility of linguists. By so doing they can help native speakers to record their traditions, and often extend the use of a language by a generation or two. Describing languages is also the only way to learn linguistics properly; one must serve an appropriate apprenticeship to master an art or profession.[12]

I recall that when I first attended lectures in linguistics, and studied the various theories of the day, I thought I understood it all pretty well. But I did feel the need to do field work. When I got out into the field (in Australia) I found that I actually understood very little about how language is structured. But I learnt, little by little, by undertaking analysis of texts, attempting grammatical generalisations, and checking these with speakers. And then the theoretical ideas that I had read about took on a new light, as I began to understand their relevance to the task I was engaged in.

There is a tradition of *not doing* field work among many modern-day linguists. Many professors dissuade their students from undertaking it; and if the students were to persist, most of the teachers would be unqualified to supervise their work. But if linguistics is to get back on track there must be an estrangement between generations. Nancy Dorian (1994: 799), discussing the need to document endangered languages, stated: 'Arguably the single most fundamental obstacle . . . is an absence of mobilizing will on the part of the profession. A case could be made, it seems to me, for great benefit in at least two different respects from making it a professional requirement that

---

[12] Besides the formalists, there is another group that has sprung up recently, who can be called 'armchair typologists'. They eschew formalisms but have never worked intensively on a language. Lacking the necessary apprenticeship, they don't have the appropriate understanding of how languages work or the ability to distinguish between reliable and unreliable grammars. They consult grammars, and make an essay at typological generalisations; but their results are frequently naive and unenlightening.

Ph.D. candidates in linguistics and Linguistic Anthropology undertake a descriptive study of an undocumented or only minimally documented language as a dissertation topic.' Young linguists must seek out departments that have experienced descriptive linguists who can supervise their field work and grammatical analysis. Indeed, if every linguistics student (and faculty member) in the world today worked on just one language that is in need of study, the prospects for full documentation of endangered languages (before they fade away) would be rosy. I doubt if one linguist in twenty is doing this.

There are other errors of attitude. One is that linguistic theorising should be largely deductive. Someone suggests a 'general property of language' (based on their knowledge of, say, English, German and Italian) and then publishes it as a theoretical advance. They then spend years trying to explain away why other languages do not fit easily into the idea. In fact, the most profitable theoretical work is inductive.[13] One studies a certain feature or correlation of features across a wide selection of languages (from every family and every linguistic area) and sees what patterns emerge. These can form the basis for a hypothesis, which should be thoroughly verified across a further selection of languages (chosen on the grounds that they have critical properties with respect to the hypothesis),[14] before being elevated to the status of a theoretical postulate.

---

[13] Bloomfield (1933: 20) remarked: 'The only useful generalizations about language are inductive generalizations. Features which we think ought to be universal may be absent from the very next language that becomes accessible . . . The fact that some features are, at any rate, widespread, is worthy of notice and calls for an explanation; when we have adequate data about many languages, we shall have to return to the problem of general grammar and to explain these similarities and divergences, but this study, when it comes, will not be speculative but inductive.'

[14] For example, the correlations described in §9.1 – between head/dependent marking and types of adjective class – are based on an examination of the grammars of about 300 languages (I actually looked at over 500 grammars, but they did not all include the relevant information). There was no 'sampling technique' involved; I simply consulted *every* available grammar in the libraries I had access to.

There are 2,000 or 3,000 languages, for which we have no decent description, that will pass into disuse within the next few generations. Trained linguists are urgently needed to document them. In some cases native speakers can be trained as linguists but in many instances an outsider is required. All this costs money. If one can hire a properly trained linguist – someone who has already written a grammar as a Ph.D. dissertation and has a thorough grounding in Basic Theory – they will need salary for themselves and for their language consultants; travel funds; equipment; facilities for writing up the description, producing a dictionary and volume of texts; and so on. At least 3 years is needed to do a good job; the total cost will be (at 1997 values) around $US200,000.

If this work is not done soon it can never be done. Future generations will then look back at the people who call themselves 'linguists' at the close of the twentieth and beginning of the twenty-first century, with bewilderment and disdain.

As already stated, good descriptive work is a prerequisite for comparative linguistics. Work is urgently needed to distinguish between types of linguistic similarity that are indicative of genetic relationships, and those likely to be due to diffusion. We need to study diffusion areas that evolved during past periods of equilibrium, and look for indicators of the past relationships between – and origins of – different peoples.

🔟 Summary and prospects

10.1 The punctuated equilibrium model

The hypothesis put forward here is that, during most of the 100,000 years or more that language has been in existence, there has been an equilibrium situation within each geographical area. A number of small political groups, each with its own language or dialect, lived in a stable situation, in relative harmony with each other. There was no large-scale hierarchical organisation and no one group or language or dialect was accorded prestige over more than a local area (or for more than a limited time).

Things were never static. Languages and political groupings are always in a state of shift. There is a steady ebb and flow. Some languages would fall out of use and others might split into two; but this would happen on a modest scale.

In each area, linguistic features of all kinds would diffuse. The languages in the area, and in regions within the area, would become more like each other in phonological systems, grammatical categories, perhaps also in lexemes and, at a slower rate, in grammatical forms. They would converge towards a linguistic prototype for the area.

Then the state of equilibrium was punctuated. This could be due to a natural happening, or to some material innovation (most notably, the introduction of agriculture), or to the emergence of an aggressive political leader or an aggressive religion. Or to the movement of a language group away from its original area into a new and unpopulated region.

A period of punctuation is typically accompanied by expansion and split. The 'family tree' model of linguistic relationship appropriately models what happens during a punctuation period, when a number of languages diverge from a common proto-language (or proto-group of languages, with convergent profiles). Eventually, equilibrium will again be established.

No equilibrium situation ever has been or ever could be observed by a scientist (although it can readily be reconstructed for Australia, and probably also for other parts of the world). The intrusion of a society that has scientists (with writing, and so on) serves as punctuation. It is because of this that the idea of an equilibrium situation between languages has not previously been posited, in this way.

Recent centuries – featuring white invasions and developments in communication – have brought equilibrium areas all over the world to an abrupt punctuation. This has led to unprecedented language losses which are currently increasing and will continue until there is just one language for each nation, eventually leading – if things remain as they are at present – to just one language for the whole world.

This essay has been programmatic, suggesting that the punctuated equilibrium model is an appropriate one to describe and explain language development in a global context. The hypothesis has been presented as a basis for future research. The ideas suggested here will need to be refined and further articulated, after work by a range of specialists on linguistic areas across the world.

10.2 Concerning comparative linguistics

The important point being made is that 'family tree' is only one of several interrelated models needed to explain linguistic relationships and development over the past 100,000 or so years. It is applicable to situations during periods of punctuation.[1] In the long

---

[1] Historical linguists have suggested that the comparative method is only workable up to a limited time-depth. Nichols (1992: 5–6) gives a period of about 8,000 years, but many scholars would opt for a shorter period (perhaps 5,000 years).

periods of equilibrium between punctuation the original family-tree relationships between languages are gradually eroded as diffusion becomes the major factor in change.

There is need to conceive of a language family having its beginnings not in the end-point of an earlier family tree but in the linguistic situation that would hold at the end of a period of equilibrium. Rather than a proto-language there may have been a proto-linguistic-area, involving a small number of languages with considerable similarities of structures and forms (but still distinct languages, on the criterion of intelligibility). And if a family did emanate from a single proto-language, as might sometimes be the case, it must be borne in mind that the proto-language would have the full characteristics of a human language, with the likelihood of suppletions, irregularities and substrata.

It is easier to prove genetic relationship between a group of languages in some circumstances than in others. The ideal situation is with languages of a generally agglutinative structure, with lexemes and grammatical forms that are mostly polysyllabic. With a group of isolating languages, or languages with many very short morphemes (one syllable or perhaps just one segment in extent), there is less prospect of confidently proving a genetic relationship and reconstructing a substantial part of the proto-system.

Subgrouping within a language family is a difficult task; only some of the splits that took place are likely to be retrievable. In particular, care must be taken to distinguish similarities between languages due to geographical contiguity and areal diffusion from those due to shared genetic inheritance.

In many situations it is impossible to tell whether a certain similarity between languages has an areal or a genetic origin. In the

This is compatible with my suggestion that family trees (for which the comparative method is relevant) are only applicable during periods of punctuation, which will not be likely to last longer than 5,000–8,000 years, and will often last for a much shorter time.

present state of linguistics the only honest answer to some questions is 'we don't know' (or 'we don't yet know'). To attempt to provide a definite answer to a question of this type takes credence away from the value of definite answers that can be provided for other questions.

Work that is needed in comparative linguistics is:

(a) For each group of languages, consider to what extent the family tree model, or the areal diffusion model, or what sort of combination of the two, is appropriate. (Such a reconsideration is needed most urgently in Sub-Saharan Africa.[2])
(b) Once the reconsideration under (a) has been completed, reconstruct as much as possible of the proto-system(s) for the proto-language or proto-linguistic-area for each putative genetic group. There are more than 200 language families currently posited across the world. These possible genetic relationships must be either fully proved – by reconstructing proto-system(s) and the systematic changes by which modern languages have developed from them – or discarded.

The following caveats should always be borne in mind:

(i) It will never be possible to fully reconstruct a proto-language or proto-linguistic-area. At best we can achieve an approximation. (Its relationship to the actual proto-language may be rather like that between an Identikit representation that the police produce of someone who has committed a crime, from what observers can describe of them, and that person themself.)

---

[2] There are so many languages in Africa that it is difficult to perceive order and organisation in the linguistic situation there. The 'Niger-Congo' and 'Nilo-Saharan' ideas have certainly been beneficial as a way of organising what is known about these languages. Now these ideas should be restudied, to see which parts of them do model genetic connection and which parts essentially describe areal relationships.

(ii) It is not a sensible policy to try to compare the original proto-languages of language families, and attempt to reconstruct a proto-proto- tableau. Firstly, we have only an approximate idea of what a proto-language was like. Secondly, it may not have been one language, but instead a group of languages. And thirdly, proto-languages or proto-linguistic-situations are likely to be the product of diffusional convergence, at the end of a period of equilibrium, rather than languages which result from a family-tree-type expansion and split.

Over the history of language development it is likely that we have had a sequence of divergence (family-tree-type splits within a short period of punctuation), then convergence (diffusion within a linguistic area during a long period of equilibrium), then divergence, then convergence, and so on. The seeds for a period of divergence lie in the end-point of a period of convergence, and vice versa.

It should scarcely need to be said that it is unlikely that it will ever be possible to decide, on linguistic grounds, whether language developed just once (monogenesis) or more than once (polygenesis). And it will certainly never be possible for linguists to recover the structure of 'proto-World' (or of 'proto-World$_1$', 'proto-World$_2$', etc.) despite the expectations of some archaeologists and geneticists – and the media – that we should be able to.

10.3 Concerning descriptive linguistics

Lists of the world's languages include 5,000–6,000 names. They generally give about 250 languages for Australia. This is a reasonable estimate for the number of languages spoken at the time of the white invasion – but over 100 languages are now dead while another 100 are moving towards extinction; no more than about 20 languages are being learnt by children. The same story is repeated world-wide. There was a recent proposal to produce a language atlas of Tanzania but 'the authorities who were approached insisted that producing a language map was not to be considered a research priority since so many languages were dying out in favour of Kiswahili, the national and official language of Tanzania, and for this reason language boundaries were changing so rapidly that such a language map might well be inapplicable within a few years' (Brenzinger, Heine and Sommer 1991: 19–20). There may be around 4,000 languages actually spoken today, but the number is steadily decreasing. Languages are falling out of use, across the world, at the rate of several dozen each year.

Each language encapsulates the world-view of its speakers – how they think, what they value, what they believe in, how they classify the world around them, how they order their lives. Once a language dies, a part of human culture is lost – for ever.

The most important task in linguistics today – indeed, the only really important task – is to get out in the field and describe languages, while this can still be done. Self-admiration in the looking glass of formalist theory can wait; that will always be possible. Linguistic description must be undertaken now.[3]

Language description is important for many reasons, including:

(a) To gain a full picture of the typological possibilities across human languages, and the correlations between their components (and between grammatical categories and the parameters – social, economic, etc. – of life-style).

(b) To provide the basic input to comparative work. In Africa and New Guinea and South America some languages are known only from a short word list. Yet they are solemnly placed within a genetic classification on this basis. The proof of genetic

---

[3] In the last few years there has been increased attention to the question of 'endangered languages' with a number of symposia on the topic and even societies formed to 'gather information'. There is only one thing that really needs to be done – *get out there and describe a language*! My general impression is that a fair proportion of the people concerned about this issue do little besides talk; they are not even thinking about undertaking field work themselves.

relationship depends most heavily on grammatical forms. A full grammatical description – together with a dictionary – for each language is necessary before they can be compared in a meaningful way and the possibility of a genetic relationship systematically investigated.

(c) Describing a minority language – and producing primers for use in schools, etc. – can help slow down (but not halt or reverse) the path of a language towards extinction. And it can help provide a better self-image for the speakers as they adjust to life in a modern, large-scale cosmopolitan world.

Language description should be undertaken by linguists who have had a thorough professional training, and not left to missionaries (as is largely the case at present). And those missionaries who do undertake language description should receive much more training and be provided with much more supervision than at present.[4]

10.4 Concerning languages

In every part of the world, the prestige language or dialect of a given area is being used more and more, with non-prestige languages and dialects being used less and less. In some situations the change in use is slight and almost indiscernible; in others it is considerable and obvious. But this change is always there.

Thus, within Brittany, Breton is being used less and less and French more and more. And in the context of global communication, English – the language with the greatest current international prestige – is being used to an increasing extent, while the use of other languages, such as French, is declining.

---

[4] Countries which do allow linguistic missionaries to work among their indigenous peoples should pay close attention to the type of people undertaking this work, and monitor how they behave. As noted in §8, some missionaries respect the indigenous culture and see themselves as offering Christianity as an additional option for the people. Others attempt to suppress traditional religion, culture, songs, etc., and replace them with their own brand of 'Christianity'.

As already mentioned, a high proportion of the speakers of a non-prestige language will also know the prestige language of the area, as a second language. The reverse is not the case. Consider a small indigenous group (in any continent) of, say, a few hundred or a few thousand people. They use their own language in daily life but they also know the lingua franca, which is employed in all contact with the general life of the nation they live in. Their own language may be used 90% of the time and the lingua franca 10%. As their degree of contact with the outside world increases, these proportions may gradually shift. Once the lingua franca is used more than 50% of the time, it will soon (within one generation or less) jump to 100%. This is the language that can be used in every aspect of life. And the indigenous language will not continue as a second language (for more than a few generations); it will fairly soon fall into disuse.

This is what is happening all over the world. Every non-prestige language is gradually being used less and less. (An exception may be a minority language of one nation which is in fact the national language of a neighbouring country, e.g. Swedish in Finland.) The process is slow but inexorable; all these languages are moving towards disuse.

The process of language loss can be – and, in a few places, is being – slowed, through the attention of linguists, or educationalists, or missionaries with the appropriate attitude; or through the concern and efforts of the people themselves. But, as an empirical observation, it can never be halted and certainly not reversed. Note too that there is no example known of a truly dead language ever being revived.

It is also the case that all over the world regional and social dialects are converging on the 'standard' form of the language. New languages evolve from diverging dialects but dialects are now converging. Not only are languages being lost at a steady rate but no new languages are evolving or seem likely to evolve (save through creolisation).

The languages that will survive are the prestige languages of each nation. The making of small nations out of big ones – for instance, Latvia and Kazakhstan – will be of immense assistance for the maintenance of their languages. We do of course have languages with millions or tens of millions of speakers which are not the sole national language of their nation, e.g. Igbo and Marathi. These are plainly not threatened in the short or medium term. But they may well be in the longer term.[5] If countries like Nigeria and India were to follow the lead of the Soviet Union and split into a number of smaller nations, each with one main language, this would enhance the chances of these languages continuing to be spoken for the longest possible time. (Speakers of Igbo did of course attempt this, with the formation of Biafra, and they fought a war over it from 1967 until 1970. But, in the end, the central government of Nigeria won.)

The only real way for a small language to survive is for its speakers to remain in isolation from the rest of the world – in the jungles of New Guinea or South America. There are a few such groups left. But 'civilisation' is steadily encroaching into all of these areas. Soon there will be no groups not in regular contact with the mainstream of life in the country in which they are situated.

The equilibrium situation has been punctuated right across the world and there is no indication that equilibrium will – or can – ever be restored. The world would have to change in a radical way for the prerequisites to be met – small egalitarian groups, living in a stable situation, in relative harmony with each other, without any particular prestige being attached to any one group or language or dialect.

If the world continues on its present course even the situation of 'one language for each nation' may not be the ending point. Globalisation is increasing. For instance, communication is expanding in scope but becoming more restrictive in medium. Russians in Russia talk to colleagues in other parts of the world by electronic

---

[5] A sad lesson that has been learnt from the study of language-death situations is that a community does not realise its language is threatened until it is too late to do anything to remedy the situation. (See Dixon 1991b: 253.)

mail – in Russian, but using the Roman alphabet (because the Internet is not designed to handle Cyrillic script).[6] In a relatively small nation such as Sweden an increasing number of people speak, read and write English of good quality. Indeed, most Ph.D. theses at Swedish universities are submitted in English. But not too many native speakers of English know any Swedish.

If things don't change, the ultimate end to the period of linguistic punctuation that we are in now will be a single world language – that which has the greatest prestige. It will take a few hundred years to get there, but this is the ultimate situation we are moving towards.

However, things may change.

[6] The French try most assiduously to preserve (and extend) the areas of use of their language. Yet in what is looked upon as one of the most go-ahead linguistics departments (in Lyon), students in all years take a course assisting them to understand linguistic works written in English. This is a realistic strategy, acknowledging the steady movement towards English as the language of international communication.

Appendix – Where the comparative method discovery procedure fails

The term 'comparative method' has been used in two distinct ways. In its original and widest sense it refers to a method of proving genetic relationships between languages. This involves the systematic comparison of grammatical forms and lexemes, establishing correspondence sets between phonemes, putting forward hypotheses concerning a putative proto-system and the changes through which the systems of modern languages developed (see, for example, Meillet 1925/1967).

'Comparative method' has also been used, in a narrower sense, to describe a set of discovery procedures which would automatically reconstruct the phonemes for a proto-language. This procedure was first put forth by Hoenigswald (1950), being directly analogised from the discovery procedures then in fashion for working out phonemes in synchronic linguistic analysis. Hoenigswald suggested that just as phonetically related phones that are in complementary distribution can be grouped together as allophones of one phoneme (as was believed at the time), so phonetically similar correspondence sets that are in complementary distribution should be grouped together as reflexes of a single proto-phoneme.

Hoenigswald's discovery procedure for comparative reconstruction rapidly gained acceptance. His own textbook (Hoenigswald 1960) stated the environment for a correspondence set in terms of other correspondence sets and looked for the grouping into proto-phonemes that gives the simplest overall phonemic system for the proto-language; there is an analogy to phonemic procedures but Hoenigswald did now imply that it is a problem of a different type from synchronic analysis. However, Hockett, in his textbook (1958:

485–505), went one step further and explained reconstruction by 'the comparative method' as if it were identical to an exercise in synchronic phonemic analysis; each distinct correspondence set relates to a phone in the proto-language and these are then grouped into phonemes in the familiar way. Anttila, in his seminal textbook (1972), describes the comparative method essentially as a discovery procedure but in a way more akin to Hoenigswald than to Hockett.

The first point to note is that the idea of being able to establish the phonemes of a language through application of a discovery procedure is an illusion. First of all, no one ever has fully worked out the phonemes of a language in this way. Secondly, it is a flawed procedure, depending on assumptions that few (or no) languages comply with. For instance, it depends on the assumption that two phonemes may never have overlapping realisations. But they often do. Consider:

/i/ realised as [i] after a palatal consonant
     and as [e] elsewhere
/ɛ/ realised as [e] after a palatal consonant
     and as [ɛ] elsewhere

Considering just the phones, and their distribution, we find:

[i] after a palatal consonant
[e] in all environments
[ɛ] except after a palatal consonant

Here [i] and [e] are in contrastive distribution since they both occur after palatal consonants, and must relate to separate phonemes. The same applies for [e] and [ɛ]. We do have [i] and [ɛ] in complementary distribution but these sounds are not phonetically adjacent and could not be considered as allophones of one phoneme. Thus, the phonemic solution of this phonetic data, applying the discovery procedure, requires three phonemes, which is wrong.

Similar difficulties arise when this discovery procedure is applied in reconstruction. We can illustrate with two examples. The

first involves conditioned changes in each of two related languages, A
and B:

in A: $*d > t$ finally   in B: $*t > d$ medially

We then have:

(1)

proto-phoneme	reflex in A	reflex in B	distribution		
			initial	medial	final
$*t$	t	t	x		x
$*t$	t	d		x	
$*d$	t	d			x
$*d$	d	d	x	x	

There are three correspondence sets, $t{:}t$, $t{:}d$ and $d{:}d$. Each is in
contrastive distribution with the others – $t{:}t$ with $t{:}d$ finally, $t{:}t$ with
$d{:}d$ initially, and $t{:}d$ with $d{:}d$ medially. We must thus reconstruct
three proto-phonemes, one for each correspondence set. This is the
wrong solution. What was needed, of course, was to split the correspondence set $t{:}d$ into two parts – those in medial position need to be
grouped with $t{:}t$ and those in final position with $d{:}d$.

Now consider an example where there is a conditioned change
in A but an unconditioned change in B (here j represents a lamino-
palatal stop):

in A: $*d > j$ before i in B: $*j > d$ everywhere

We then get:

(2)

proto-phoneme	reflex in A	reflex in B	environment	reconstruction
$*d$	d	d	except before $i{:}i$	$*d$
$*d$	j	d	before $i{:}i$	$*j$
$*j$	j	d	everywhere	

We have two correspondence sets, *d:d* and *j:d*; *j:d* occurs everywhere and *d:d* everywhere except before *i:i*, so they are in contrastive distribution. Each must relate to a proto-phoneme, presumably **d* for *d:d* and **j* for *j:d*. This gives the correct number of phonemes but assigns them in the wrong way. The middle line of (2) comes from **d* but is wrongly assigned to **j*. And note that this wrong solution cannot be improved in the way that (1) could be (by distinguishing between the medial and final occurrences of *t:d*). Some of the correspondence sets *j:d* that occur before *i:i* come from **d*, but some of them also come from **j*, in the third line of (2). There is no way to disentangle these sets.

Hoenigswald did perceive some of these potential difficulties to the efficient operation of the discovery procedures he was suggesting (1960: 124ff.), but his caveats have largely gone unremarked by later expositors. Of course, comparing more than just two languages would lessen – but by no means eliminate – the potentiality for getting wrong results by applying this procedure.

It will be seen that the comparative method discovery procedure will only yield a correct reconstruction if certain conditions have applied to the changes that have taken place between the proto-language and modern languages – and we have no way of knowing whether or not these conditions have been complied with.

This should serve to indicate the tentative nature of any attempt to reconstruct a proto-system. And the speculative nature of trying to relate together language families by comparing reconstructed proto-systems and proto-forms. As suggested throughout this essay, language families generally evolve during a period of punctuation but have their origin in the end portion of a period of equilibrium. It is neither sensible nor provident to look for a family tree of family trees.

References

Adelaar, Willem F. H. 1989. Review of Greenberg, 1987, in *Lingua*, 78.249–55.

Aikhenvald, Alexandra Y. 1996. 'Areal diffusion in north-west Amazonia: The case of Tariana', *Anthropological Linguistics*, 38.73–116.

—— Forthcoming. 'The Arawak language family', to appear in Dixon and Aikhenvald, forthcoming.

Aikhenvald, Alexandra Y. and Dixon, R. M. W. Forthcoming. 'Evidentials and areal typology: A case study from Amazonia', to appear in *Language Sciences*.

Alpher, Barry. 1994. 'Yir-Yoront ideophones', pp. 161–78 of Hinton, Nichols and Ohala, 1994.

Alpher, Barry and Nash, David. Ms. 1996. 'Lexical replacement and cognate equilibrium in Australia'.

Anttila, Raimo. 1972. *An introduction to comparative and historical linguistics*. New York: Macmillan. (Second edition: 1989. Amsterdam: John Benjamins.)

Archer, W. G. 1943. 'The heron will not twist his moustache', *Journal of the Bihar and Orissa Research Society*, 29.55–73.

Arndt, Walter W. 1959. 'The performance of glottochronology in German', *Language*, 35.180–92.

Arnol'd, V. I. 1992. *Catastrophe theory*, third edition. Berlin: Springer-Verlag.

Austin, Peter. 1981. 'Switch-reference in Australia', *Language*, 57.309–34.

Bakker, Peter and Mous, Maarten (eds.) 1994. *Mixed languages: 15 case studies in language intertwining*. Amsterdam: Institute for Functional Research into Language and Language Use.

Baldi, Philip (ed.) 1990. *Linguistic change and reconstruction methodology*. Berlin: Mouton de Gruyter.

Ballard, W. L. 1985. 'The linguistic history of South China: Miao-Yao and southern dialects', pp. 58–84 of *Linguistics of the Sino-Tibetan area: The state of the art*, edited by Graham Thurgood, James Matisoff and David Bradley. Canberra: Pacific Linguistics.

Barnes, Janet. 1984. 'Evidentials in the Tuyuca verb', *International Journal of American Linguistics*, 50.255–71.

Barth, Fredrik (ed.) 1969. *Ethnic groups and boundaries: The social organization*

of culture difference. Bergen: Universitets Forlaget; London: Allen and
Unwin; and Boston: Little, Brown.

Bellwood, Peter. 1991. 'The Austronesian dispersal and the origin of languages',
Scientific American, 265(1).88–93.

1996. 'The origins and spread of agriculture in the Indo-Pacific region:
Gradualism and diffusion or revolution and colonization', pp. 465–98 of
Harris, 1996.

Beneviste, Emile. 1966. *Problèmes de linguistique générale.* Paris: Gallimard.

Bergslund, Knut and Vogt, Hans. 1962. 'On the validity of glottochronology',
Current Anthropology, 3.115–58.

Berman, Howard. 1992. 'A comment on the Yurok and Kalapayu data in
Greenberg's *Languages in the Americas*', *International Journal of American
Linguistics*, 58.230–3.

Birdsell, Joseph B. 1957. 'Some population problems involving pleistocene man',
Cold Spring Harbor Symposia on Quantitative Biology, 22.47–69.

1977. 'The recalibration of a paradigm for the first peopling of Greater
Australia', pp. 113–67 of *Sunda and Sahul: Prehistoric studies in Southeast
Asia, Melanesia and Australia*, edited by Jim Allen, Jack Golson and Rhys
Jones. London: Academic Press.

Birnbaum, Henrik. 1977. *Linguistic reconstruction: Its potential and limitations
in new perspective.* Monograph of *Journal of Indo-European Studies*.

Bloomfield, Leonard. 1933. *Language.* New York: Holt, Rinehart and Winston.

Breen, Gavan. 1990. *Salvage studies of western Queensland Aboriginal languages.*
Canberra: Pacific Linguistics.

Brenzinger, Matthias; Heine, Bernd and Sommer, Gabriele. 1991. 'Language death
in Africa', pp. 19–44 of Robins and Uhlenbeck, 1991.

Butlin, N. G. 1989. 'The palaeoeconomic history of Aboriginal migration',
Australian Economic History Review, 29.1–57.

Callaghan, Catherine A. and Miller, Wick R. 1962. 'Swadesh's Macro Mixtecan
hypothesis and English', *Southwestern Journal of Anthropology*, 18.278–85.

Campbell, Lyle. 1977. *Quichean linguistic prehistory* (University of California
Publications in Linguistics 81). Berkeley and Los Angeles: University of
California Press.

1988. Review of Greenberg, 1987, in *Language*, 64.591–615.

1990. 'Indo-European and Uralic trees', *Diachronica*, 7.149–80.

1993. 'On proposed universals of grammatical borrowing', pp. 91–109 of
*Historical linguistics 1989: Papers from the 9th International Conference on
Historical Linguistics*, edited by Henk Aertsen and Robert J. Jeffers.
Amsterdam: John Benjamins.

Forthcoming-a. 'Nostratic: A personal assessment', to appear in *Nostratic:*

Evidence and status, edited by Brian Joseph and Joe Salmons. Amsterdam: John Benjamins.

Forthcoming-b. 'On the linguistic prehistory of Finno-Ugric', to appear in *Festschrift for Jacek Fisiak*, edited by Raymond Hickey. Berlin: Mouton de Gruyter.

Campbell, Lyle; Kaufman, Terrence and Smith-Stark, Thomas C. 1986. 'Meso-America as a linguistic area', *Language*, 62.530–70.

Caspar, Franz. 1956. *Tupari*. London: Bell.

Chafe, Wallace. 1987. Review of Greenberg, 1987, in *Current Anthropology*, 28.652–3.

Chafe, Wallace and Nichols, Johanna (eds.) 1986. *Evidentiality: The linguistic coding of epistemology*. Norwood, N.J.: Ablex.

Chappell, J.; Omura, Akio and Esat, Tezer *et al.* 1996. 'Reconciliation of late Quaternary sea levels derived from coral terraces at Huon Peninsula with deep sea level oxygen isotope records', *Earth and Planetary Science Letters*, 141.227–36.

Collinder, Björn. 1965. *An introduction to the Uralic languages*. Berkeley and Los Angeles: University of California Press.

Comrie, Bernard. 1989. 'Genetic classification, contact and variation', pp. 81–93 of *Synchronic and diachronic approaches to linguistic variation and change* (Georgetown University Round Table on Languages and Linguistics 1988), edited by Thomas J. Walsh. Washington, D.C.: Georgetown University Press.

Coomaraswamy, Ananda K. 1949. *The bugbear of literacy*. London: Dennis Dobson. (Published in the USA: 1943. *Am I my brother's keeper?* New York: John Day.)

DeLancey, Scott. 1985. 'The analysis–synthesis cycle in Tibeto-Burman: A case study in motivated change', pp. 367–89 of *Iconicity in syntax*, edited by John Haiman. Amsterdam: John Benjamins.

Dench, Alan C. 1982. 'The development of an accusative case marking pattern in the Ngayarda languages of Western Australia', *Australian Journal of Linguistics*, 2.43–59.

1995. *Martuthunira: A language of the Pilbara region of Western Australia*. Canberra: Pacific Linguistics.

Dixon, R. M. W. 1972. *The Dyirbal language of North Queensland*. Cambridge: Cambridge University Press.

1977. *A grammar of Yidiɲ*. Cambridge: Cambridge University Press.

1980. *The languages of Australia*. Cambridge: Cambridge University Press.

1982. *Where have all the adjectives gone? and other essays in semantics and syntax*. Berlin: Mouton.

1988. *A grammar of Boumaa Fijian*. Chicago: University of Chicago Press.

1991a. 'Some observations on the grammar of Indian English', pp. 437–47 of *Studies in Dravidian and general linguistics: A festschrift for Bh. Krishnamurti*, edited by B. Lakshmi Bai and B. Ramakrishna Reddy. Hyderabad, India: Osmania University.

1991b. 'The endangered languages of Australia, Indonesia and Oceania', pp. 229–55 of Robins and Uhlenbeck, 1991.

1991c. 'Mbabaram', pp. 348–402 of *Handbook of Australian languages*, Vol. 4, edited by R. M. W. Dixon and B. J. Blake. Melbourne: Oxford University Press.

1994. *Ergativity*. Cambridge: Cambridge University Press.

Forthcoming. *Australian languages:* Vol. 1 – *Their nature and development;* Vol. 2 – *A comprehensive catalog*. Cambridge: Cambridge University Press.

Dixon, R. M. W. and Aikhenvald, Alexandra Y. (eds.) Forthcoming. *Amazonian languages*. Cambridge: Cambridge University Press.

Dorian, Nancy C. 1994. Review of Robins and Uhlenbeck, 1991, in *Language*, 70.797–802.

Eldredge, Niles and Gould, Stephen Jay. 1972. 'Punctuated equilibria: An alternative to phyletic gradualism', pp. 82–115 of *Models in paleobiology*, edited by T. J. M. Schopf. San Francisco: Freeman, Cooper.

Embleton, Sheila. 1992. 'Historical linguistics: Mathematical concepts', pp. 131–5 of *International encyclopedia of linguistics*, Vol. 2, edited by William Bright. New York: Oxford University Press.

Emeneau, Murray B. 1956. 'India as a linguistic area', *Language*, 32.3–16. (Reprinted in Hymes, 1964, pp. 642–53.)

1980. *Language and linguistic area: Essays by Murray B. Emeneau*, selected and introduced by Anwar S. Dil. Stanford: Stanford University Press.

Foley, William A. 1986. *The Papuan languages of New Guinea*. Cambridge: Cambridge University Press.

Ford, Lysbeth. Forthcoming. 'A grammar of Emmi, a language of the Northern Territory of Australia'. Ph.D. thesis, Australian National University.

Fujioka, Katsuji. 1908. *Nihongo no ichi*. (Reprinted in *Nihongo no Keitō – Kihonronbunshū* 1, edited by S. Shiba *et al.* 1985. Osaka: Izumishoin, pp. 60–85.)

Goddard, Ives. 1990. Review of Greenberg, 1987, in *Linguistics*, 28.556–8.

Golovko, Evgenij. 1994. 'Mednyj Aleut or Copper Island Aleut: An Aleut–Russian mixed language', pp. 113–21 of Bakker and Mous, 1994.

Goodenough, Ward H. 1992. 'Gradual and quantum changes in the history of Chuukese (Trukese) phonology', *Oceanic Linguistics*, 31.93–114.

References

Greenberg, Joseph H. 1957. *Essays in linguistics*. Chicago: University of Chicago Press.

1963. *The languages of Africa*. Bloomington: Indiana University Research Center in Anthropology, Folklore and Culture.

1971. 'The Indo-Pacific hypothesis', pp. 807–71 of *Current trends in linguistics*, Vol. VIII – *Linguistics in Oceania*, edited by Thomas A. Sebeok. The Hague: Mouton.

1987. *Language in the Americas*. Stanford: Stanford University Press.

1989. 'Classification of American Indian languages: A reply to Campbell', *Language*, 65.107–14.

Gudschinsky, Sarah. 1956. 'The ABCs of lexicostatistics (glottochronology)', *Word*, 12.175–210. (Reprinted in Hymes, 1964, pp. 612–23.)

Gumperz, John J. and Wilson, Robert. 1971. 'Convergence and creolisation: A case from the Indo-Aryan/Dravidian border', pp. 151–67 of *Pidginisation and creolisation of languages*, edited by Dell Hymes. Cambridge: Cambridge University Press.

Haas, Mary R. 1969. *The prehistory of languages*. The Hague: Mouton.

Hale, Kenneth L. 1971. 'A note on a Walbiri tradition of antonymy', pp. 472–82 of *Semantics: An interdisciplinary reader in philosophy, linguistics and psychology*, edited by Danny D. Steinberg and Leon A. Jakobovits. Cambridge: Cambridge University Press.

1973. 'Deep-surface canonical disparities in relation to analysis and change: An Australian example', pp. 401–58 of *Current trends in linguistics*, Vol. XI – *Diachronic, areal and typological linguistics*, edited by Thomas A. Sebeok. The Hague: Mouton.

Hall, Robert A. 1950. 'The reconstruction of proto-Romance', *Language*, 26.6–27.

1976. *Comparative Romance grammar: 2. Proto-Romance phonology*. New York: American Elsevier.

1983. *Proto-Romance morphology*. Amsterdam: John Benjamins.

Hansen, K. C. 1984. 'Communicability of some Western Desert communalects', pp. 1–112 of *Language survey*, edited by Joyce Hudson and Noreen Pym. Darwin: Summer Institute of Linguistics, Australian Aboriginal Branch.

Harris, David R. (ed.). 1996. *The origins and spread of agriculture and pastoralism in Eurasia*. London: UCL Press.

Harrisson, Tom. 1937. *Savage civilisation*. London: Gollancz.

Hashimoto, Mantaro J. 1976a. 'The agrarian and pastoral diffusion of languages', pp. 1–14 of *Genetic relationship, diffusion and typological similarities of East and South East Asian languages*, edited by Mantaro J. Hashimoto. Tokyo.

1976b. 'Language diffusion on the Asian continent: Problems of typological diversity in Sino-Tibetan', *Computational Analysis of Asian and African Languages*, 3.49–66.

Haudricourt, A. G. 1961. 'Bipartition et tripartition des systèmes de tons dans quelques langages d'Extrême-Orient', *Bulletin de la Société Linguistique de Paris*, 56.163–80.

Heath, Jeffrey. 1978. *Linguistic diffusion in Arnhem Land*. Canberra: Australian Institute of Aboriginal Studies.

Hemming, John. 1978. *Red gold: The conquest of the Brazilian Indians*, 1500–1760. Cambridge, Mass.: Harvard University Press.

Hinton, Leanne; Nichols, Johanna and Ohala, John J. 1994. *Sound symbolism*. Cambridge: Cambridge University Press.

Hockett, Charles F. 1958. *A course in modern linguistics*. New York: Macmillan.

Hodge, Carleton T. 1970. 'The linguistic cycle', *Language Sciences*, 13.1–7.

Hoenigswald, Henry M. 1950. 'The principal step in comparative grammar', *Language*, 26.357–64.

   1960. *Language change and linguistic reconstruction*. Chicago: University of Chicago Press.

Hoijer, Harry. 1956. 'Lexicostatistics: A critique', *Language*, 32.49–60.

Hymes, Dell (ed.) 1964. *Language in culture and society: A reader in linguistics and anthropology*. New York: Harper and Row.

Jakobson, Roman. 1962. *Selected writings, I: Phonological studies*. The Hague: Mouton.

Kachru, Braj. 1965. 'The Indianness in Indian English', *Word*, 21.391–410.

   1983. *The Indianization of English: The English language in India*. Delhi: Oxford University Press.

Kaufman, Terrence. 1990. 'Language history in South America: What we know and how to know more', pp. 13–73 of *Amazonian linguistics: Studies in lowland South American languages*, edited by Doris L. Payne. Austin: University of Texas Press.

Kimball, Geoffrey. 1992. 'A critique of Muskogean, "Gulf", and Yukian material in *Language in the Americas*', *International Journal of American Linguistics*, 58.447–501.

Kirton, Jean F. 1971. 'Complexities of Yanyula nouns: Inter-relationship of linguistics and anthropology', pp. 15–70 of *Papers in Australian Linguistics*, Vol. 5. Canberra: Pacific Linguistics.

Kirton, Jean and Charlie, Bella. 1996. *Further aspects of the grammar of Yanyuwa, northern Australia*. Canberra: Pacific Linguistics.

Krantz, Grover S. 1988. *Geographical development of European languages*. New York: Peter Lang.

Kumakhov, Mukhadin and Vamling, Karina. 1995. 'On root and subordinate clause structure in Kabardian', *Lund University Department of Linguistics Working Papers*, 44.91–110.

LaPolla, Randy. 1994. 'Parallel grammaticalizations in Tibeto-Burman languages: Evidence of Sapir's "drift"', *Linguistics of the Tibeto-Burman Area*, 17.61–80.

Leslau, Wolf. 1945. 'The influence of Cushitic on the Semitic languages of Ethiopia: A problem of substratum', *Word*, 1.59–82.

Li, Fang Kuei. 1977. *A handbook of comparative Thai* (Oceanic Linguistics Special Publications 15). Honolulu: University of Hawaii Press.

Lithgow, David. 1973. 'Language change on Woodlark Island', *Oceania*, 44.101–8.

Longacre, Robert E. 1961. 'Swadesh's Macro Mixtecan hypothesis', *International Journal of American Linguistics*, 27.9–29.

Loveday, Leo J. 1996. *Language contact in Japan: A socio-linguistic history*. Oxford: Oxford University Press.

McConvell, Patrick. 1996. 'Backtracking to Babel: The chronology of Pama-Nyungan expansion in Australia', *Archaeology in Oceania*, 31.125–44.

McGregor, William. 1990. *A functional grammar of Gooniyandi*. Amsterdam: John Benjamins.

Mallory, J. P. 1989. *In search of the Indo-Europeans: Language, archaeology and myth*. London: Thames and Hudson.

Masica, Colin P. 1976. *Defining a linguistic area: South Asia*. Chicago: University of Chicago Press.

1991. *The Indo-Aryan languages*. Cambridge: Cambridge University Press.

Matisoff, James A. 1976. 'Lahu causative constructions: Case hierarchies and the morphology/syntax cycle in a Tibeto-Burman perspective', pp. 413–42 of *Syntax and semantics 6: The grammar of causative constructions*, edited by Masayoshi Shibatani. New York: Academic Press.

1990. 'On megalocomparison', *Language*, 66.109–20.

1991. 'Areal and universal dimensions of grammatization in Lahu', pp. 383–453 of *Approaches to grammaticalization*, Vol. II, edited by Elizabeth Closs Traugott. Amsterdam: John Benjamins.

Meillet, Antoine. 1925. *La méthode comparative en linguistique historique*. Paris: Champion. (English translation: 1967. *The comparative method in historical linguistics*. Paris: Champion.)

1967. *The Indo-European dialects*, translated by Samuel N. Rosenberg. University of Alabama Press. (Original French edition published in 1908.)

Meltzer, David J. 1995. 'Clocking the first Americans', *Annual Review of Anthropology*, 24.21–45.

Merlan, Francesca. 1982. *Mangarayi* (Lingua Descriptive Series). Amsterdam: North-Holland.

Mous, Maarten. 1994. 'Ma'a or Mbugu', pp. 175–200 of Bakker and Mous, 1994.

References

Mulvaney, D. J. 1975. *The prehistory of Australia*, revised edition.
      Harmondsworth: Penguin.

Nadkarni, Mangesh V. 1975. 'Bilingualism and syntactic change in Konkani',
      Language, 51.672–83.

Nichols, Johanna. 1986. 'Head-marking and dependent-marking grammar',
      Language, 62.56–119.

   1990. 'Linguistic diversity and the first settlement of the new world', *Language*,
      66.475–521.

   1992. *Linguistic diversity in time and space*. Chicago: University of Chicago
      Press.

   1996. 'The comparative method as heuristic', pp. 39–71 of *The comparative
      method reviewed: Regularity and irregularity in language change*, edited by
      Mark Durie and Malcolm Ross. New York: Oxford University Press.

Nissen, Hans J.; Damerow, Peter and Englund, Robert K. 1993. *Archaic bookkeep-
      ing: Early writing and techniques of economic administration in the
      Ancient Near East*. Chicago: University of Chicago Press.

Norman, Jerry. 1988. *Chinese*. Cambridge: Cambridge University Press.

Olmsted, D. L. 1961. 'Lexicostatistics as "proof" of genetic relationship: The case
      of "Macro Manguean"', *Anthropological Linguistics*, 3(6).9–14.

Pawley, Andrew. 1981. 'Melanesian diversity and Polynesian homogeneity: A
      unified explanation for language change', pp. 269–309 of *Studies in Pacific
      languages and cultures in honour of Bruce Biggs*, edited by Jim Hollyman
      and Andrew Pawley. Auckland: Linguistic Society of New Zealand.

Pawley, Andrew and Ross, Malcolm. 1995. 'The prehistory of the Oceanic lan-
      guages: A current view', pp. 39–74 of *The Austronesians: Historical and
      comparative perspectives*, edited by Peter Bellwood, James J. Fox and
      Darrell Tryon. Canberra: Department of Anthropology, Research School of
      Pacific and Asian Studies, Australian National University.

Payne, David L. 1990. 'Some widespread grammatical forms in South American
      languages', pp. 75–87 of *Amazonian linguistics: Studies in lowland South
      American languages*, edited by Doris L. Payne. Austin: University of Texas
      Press.

Pedersen, Holger. 1931. *The discovery of language: Linguistic science in the nine-
      teenth century*. Cambridge, Mass.: Harvard University Press.

Rankin, Robert L. 1992. Review of Greenberg, 1987, in *International Journal of
      American Linguistics*, 58.324–51.

Reichard, Gladys A. 1940. 'Composition and symbolism of Coeur d'Alene verb
      stems', *International Journal of American Linguistics*, 11.47–63.

Renfrew, Colin. 1987. *Archaeology and language: The puzzle of Indo-European
      origins*. London: Jonathan Cape.

Robins, Robert H. and Uhlenbeck, Eugenius M. (eds.). 1991. *Endangered languages*. Oxford: Berg.

Sapir, Edward. 1921. *Language*. New York: Harcourt Brace.

Schmidt, J. 1872. *Die Verwandtischaftsverhältnisse der indogermanischen Sprachen*. Weimar: Böhlau.

Sherzer, Joel. 1976. *An areal-typological study of American Indian languages north of Mexico*. Amsterdam: North-Holland.

Shevoroshkin, Vitaly and Manaster Ramer, Alexis. 1991. 'Some recent work on the remote relationships of languages', pp. 178–99 of *Sprung from some common source*, edited by Sydney M. Lamb and E. Douglas Mitchell. Stanford: Stanford University Press.

Shibatani, Masayoshi. 1990. *The languages of Japan*. Cambridge: Cambridge University Press.

Siebert, Frank T., Jr 1967. 'The original home of the Proto-Algonquian people', pp. 13–47 of *Contributions to anthropology: Linguistics*, Vol. I. Ottawa: National Museum of Canada.

Siegel, Jeff (ed.) 1993. *Koines and koineization* (= No. 99 of *International Journal of the Sociology of Language*).

Slobin, Dan I. 1982. 'Universal and particular in the acquisition of language', pp. 128–70 of *Language acquisition: The state of the art*, edited by Eric Wanner and Lila R. Gleitman. Cambridge: Cambridge University Press.

Snyman. J.W. 1970. *An introduction to the !Xũ language*. Cape Town: Balkema.

Southworth, Franklin C. 1958. *A test of the comparative method: A historically controlled reconstruction based on four modern Indic languages*. Ph.D. dissertation, Yale University.

Stankiewicz, Edward. 1972. *A Baudouin de Courtenay anthology*. Bloomington: Indiana University Press.

Subrahmanian, K. 1978. 'Penchant for the florid', pp. 203–6 of *Indian writing in English*, edited by R. Mohan. Orient Longman.

Swadesh, Morris. 1951. 'Diffusional cumulation and archaic residue as historical explanations', *Southwestern Journal of Anthropology*, 7.1–21. (Reprinted in revised form in Hymes, 1964, pp. 624–37.)

1960. 'The Oto-Manguean hypothesis and Macro Mixtecan', *International Journal of American Linguistics*, 26.79–111.

Teeter, Karl V. 1963. 'Lexicostatistics and genetic relationship', *Language*, 39.638–48.

Thomason, Sarah Grey and Kaufman, Terrence. 1988. *Language contact, creolisation, and genetic linguistics*. Berkeley and Los Angeles: University of California Press.

Threlkeld, L. E. 1857. 'The Gospel by St Luke translated into the language of the

Awabakal'. Ms. (Published as pp. 121–94 of Threlkeld, 1892. *An Australian language as spoken by the Awabakal . . .*, edited by John Fraser. Sydney: Government Printer.)

Tindale, Norman B. and Birdsell Joseph B. 1941. 'Tasmanoid tribes in North Queensland', *Records of the South Australian Museum*, 7.1–9.

Trubetzkoy, N. S. 1939. 'Gedanken über das Indogermanenproblem', *Acta Linguistica (Hafniensa)*, 1.81–9.

Weinreich, Uriel. 1953. *Languages in contact: Findings and problems* (Publications of the Linguistic Circle of New York 1). (Reprinted: 1964. The Hague: Mouton.)

Welmers, Wm E. 1973. *African language structures*. Berkeley and Los Angeles: University of California Press.

Welmers, William E. and Welmers, Beatrice F. 1969. 'Noun modifiers in Igbo', *International Journal of American Linguistics*, 35.315–22.

Williamson, Kay. 1989. 'Niger-Congo overview', pp. 3–45 of *The Niger-Congo languages: A classification and description of Africa's largest language family*, edited by John Bendor-Samuel. Lanham, Md.: University Presses of America.

Zepeda, Ofelia and Hill, Jane H. 1991. 'The condition of Native American languages in the United States', pp. 135–55 of Robins and Uhlenbeck, 1991.

Index

'n' after a page number indicates mention in a note to that page

accidental similarity 15n
accusative system 18, 56, 93, 122n
Adelaar, Willem F. H. 34
adjective classes 124–7
African languages 17, 32–5, 49n, 95, 142
Afroasiatic family 38
agglutinative type 41–2
agriculture, introduction of 77–8, 84,
    86–7
Aikhenvald, Alexandra Y. 20n, 24, 50,
    111n, 120, 123
Aleut 12
Algonquian language family 48, 98
Alpher, Barry 27n, 64n
Altaic linguistic area 16, 32, 38
Amazonia as a linguistic area 16, 17, 84
American Indian languages 34–5, 49n
Americas 84, 86, 93–5, 119
analysis, two senses of the term 133
Anttila, Raimo 150
Arawak language family
    expansion of 84
    head marking 122
    in rainforest 88–9
    in Vaupés linguistic area 24–5, 120
    subgrouping in 50
    see also Tariana
Archer, W. G. 82n
areal influence, *see* diffusion
Aristotle 128

armchair typologists 136n
Arndt, Walter W. 36
Arnhem Land 21
Arnol'd, V. I. 75n
aspect 119
Athapaskan language family 25, 61
Austin, Peter 21
Australia 84, 87–93
Australian languages
    adjective classes 126–7
    as a linguistic area 18
    dating 48, 89–93
    50 percent vocabulary level 26–7, 71–3
    grammatical borrowing 23n
    grammatical change 57
    initial dropping 14
    language loss 107–9, 115
    lexical loans 24
    multiple synonymy 72–3
    shared vocabulary 10
    switch-reference marking 21
    syntactic marking 123–4
Austronesian family 17, 29–30, 61, 86–7
Awabakal 112

Bahasa Indonesian 80
Bakker, Peter 13n
Baldi, Philip 38n
Balkans 16, 119
Ballard, W. L. 102n

Bantu languages 11–12, 54
Barnes, Janet 120
Barth, Fredrik 68n
Basic Linguistic Theory 128–38
Bau Fijian 104–5, 114, 119, 128–30
Bellwood, Peter 77, 86
Benveniste, Emile 14
Berber languages 125
Bergslund, Knut 11, 36
Berman, Howard 34
Biafra 147
Bible translation 112–15
Biblical Hebrew 118
Bidjara 91n
Birdsell, Joseph B. 83, 87, 89
Birnbaum, Henrik 11
Bloomfield, Leonard 30n, 98n, 137n
borrowing, attitudes to 27
Boumaa Fijian 104–5
bound pronouns 55–7, 93, 123–4
Breen, Gavan 10n, 19n
Brennan, Gloria 26n
Brenzinger, Matthias 144
Breton 145
Burma 80–1n
Bushman languages 118, 119
Butlin, N. G. 87

Callaghan, Catherine A. 40
calques 20n
Campbell, Lyle 16, 20n, 34, 36, 39, 48, 100
Cantonese 7, 9n
Carib language family 84, 88–9
case systems 54–6, 121–2
Caspar, Franz 108
Catastrophe Theory 75n
Caucasian, *see* North-east Caucasias
    family, North-west Caucasias family
Chafe, Wallace 34, 119
change, modes of 54–66

change, rate of 9–10
Chappell, John 87
Charlie, Bella 113
Chinese languages 7, 9n, 16, 41, 42, 102
Christian missionaries 112–15
Chukchee 82
Classical Chinese 42
Classical Greek 119
Classical Japanese 119
clicks 17, 118
Collinder, Björn 38
comparative method 30–1, 149–52
complexity of languages 23
Comrie, Bernard 10n
constituent order 21, 33, 121-4
Coomaraswamy, Ananda K. 82n
Copper Island Aleut 12–13
core vocabulary 10–12, 20, 36–7
Courtenay, Baudouin de 13–14
creole languages 13n
Cushitic languages 11–12, 21
cycle of change 41-2

Damerow, Peter 81
Damin initiation style 13n
dating of proto-languages 46–9, 99
DeLancey, Scott 42n
Dench, Alan C. 56, 126n
dependent marking 21, 121-7
dialect chains 8
diffusion 15–27, 50–2, 71–3, 120–1
Diller, Tony 42n
Djamindjung 123
Djaru 64n
Dobu 10
Dorian, Nancy C. 136
Dravidian family 19, 25, 42
Dulong 69n
Dyirbal 105, 109
    see also Girramay, Jirrbal

Index

Egyptian 42, 46, 81
Eldredge, Niles 3
Embleton, Sheila 36
Emeneau, Murray B. 15, 16
Emmi 127
endangered languages, *see* language loss
English
  adjective class 125
  as a lingua franca 85, 145, 148n
  as a 'Macro-Mixtecan' language 40
  dialects 7–8
  language change 14, 45–6, 50, 52–3, 56,
    57, 105
Englund, Robert K. 81
equilibrium situation 68–73
ergative system 18, 56–7, 93, 122n
Ethiopia 21
Everett, Dan and Keren 82n
evidentiality 25, 119–21

family tree model 28–53
field work, exhilaration of 134
50 percent equilibrium idea 26–7, 71–3
Fijian 104–5, 114, 119, 128, 129–30
Finno-Ugric family 42
Foley, William A. 18, 88
Ford, Lysbeth 127
formalisms (non-basic theories) 131–5
French 10, 22, 52–3, 145, 148n
Fujioka, Katsuji 32
fusional type 41–2

German 14, 22, 52–3
Germanic languages 50
Girramay dialect of Dyirbal 26n
glottochronology 11, 35–7
Goddard, Ives 34
Golovko, Evgenij 12
Goodenough, Ward H. 3n
Gooniyandi 133n

Gould, Stephen Jay 3
grammatical categories, borrowing of
  20–3
grammatical forms, borrowing of 21–3
Grant, Chloe 26n, 109
Grassmann's Law 14
Greek 14, 20n, 46, 50, 119
Green, Diana 64n
Greenberg, Joseph H. 14, 32–5, 43–4,
  49n
Grimm's Law 50
Guahibo 84
Guaraní 106n
Gudschinsky, Sarah 36
Gumperz, John J. 25

Haas, Mary R. 16
Hale, Kenneth L. 13n
Hall, Robert A. 46
Hansen, K. C. 72
Harris, David R. 48
Harrisson, Tom 82n
Hashimoto, Mantaro J. 16, 102n
Haudricourt, A. G. 102n
head marking 21, 121–7
Heath, Jeffrey 21, 22n
Hebrew 46, 111, 118
Heine, Bernd 144
Hemming, John 107
Hill, Jane H. 136
Hinton, Leanne 64n
Hittite 81
Hockett, Charles F. 149–50
Hodge, Carleton T. 42
Hoenigswald, Henry M. 149, 152
Hoijer, Harry 36
Homer 81
Hong Kong 9n
Hungarian 27
Hymes, Dell 11

Icelandic 9
ideophones 64n
IE, *see* Indo-European family
Igbo 124, 147
inclusive/exclusive distinction in
    pronouns 117
incorporation 55
India 85, 147
    as a linguistic area 16–17
Indian English 53, 85
Indo-Aryan languages 19, 25, 28–9, 46, 47
Indo-European family
    and family tree model 14, 28, 31, 53
    dating of 29, 47–8
    grammatical profile 41n, 42
    proto-language 41n, 100–1
Indo-Pacific hypothesis 34, 49n
Indonesian 80
inductive approach 137
invasions 103–4
Irish 79n, 109
isolating type 41–2

Jakobson, Roman 57
Japanese 27, 32, 60–1, 119
Jarawara 68n, 111–12
Jê language family 89
Jirrbal dialect of Dyirbal 26n

Kabardian 118, 122
Kachru, Braj 53
Kalanga 80
Kannada 25
Kargan culture 47
Katz, Aya 111
Kaufman, Terrence 11–12, 16
Kazakhstan 147
Kilivila 10
Kimball, Geoffrey 34
Kirton, Jean F. 58n, 113

Kiswahili 41, 83, 144
koiné 60n
Konkani 25n
Kpelle 64n
Krantz, Grover S. 48n
Kumakhov, Mukhadin 118, 122
Kupwar village 25

language, two senses of word 7–8
language engineering 13
language loss 107–12, 116–17, 138, 143–8
language revival, impossibility of 111
language splitting 58–63
LaPolla, Randy 9n, 14, 16n, 22, 69n, 81n
Lardil 13n
Latin 10, 41, 46, 50, 121, 122n, 125
Latvia 147
Leslau, Wolf 21
lexical borrowing 19–20, 24
lexicostatistics 11, 35–7
Li, Fang Kuei 42n
linguistic area 3n, 15–27, 71–3
Lisu 22
Lithgow, David 10
Longacre, Robert E. 40
Loveday, Leo J. 27
Luxemburg 22
Lyons, John 36n

Ma'a 11–12
McConvell, Patrick 36–7n
McGregor, William 123n
Macro-Mixtecan hypothesis 40
Makú 84, 114
Malay 125
Mallory, J. P. 47
Manaster Ramer, Alexis 39
Mandarin 7, 9n
Mande languages 33
Mangarayi 124

Index

Maori 110–11
Marathi 25, 147
Masica, Colin P. 16, 19
mass comparison 33–5
Matisoff, James A. 14, 35n, 40, 42n
Matos, Rinaldo de 64n
Mbabaram 15
Mbugu 11–12
Mednyj Aleut 12–13
Meillet, Antoine 39n, 98n, 149
Meltzer, David J. 94n
merging of languages 71–3
Merlan, Francesca 124n
Meso-American linguistic area 16
Miller, Wick R. 40
missionaries, Christian 112–15
Mongolian language family 32, 38
monogenesis 66
Mous, Maarten 11–12, 13n
Mulvaney, D. J. 76n
Mura-Pirahã 84
Muyuw 10
Myanmar 80–1n

Nadkarni, Mangesh V. 25n
Nakh-Daghestanian 96
Nambikwara 84
Nash, David 27n
Navajo 110
Ndebele 79–80
negation 118
New Guinea 10, 17–18, 85–90
New Zealand 84, 86–7, 110–11
Ngayarda languages 56
Nichols, Johanna 21, 39n, 64n, 94, 119, 121n, 140n
Niger-Congo hypothesis 32–5, 142n
Nigeria 85, 147
Nigerian English 85
Nilo-Saharan hypothesis 142n

Nilotic languages 119
Nissen, Hans J. 81
Njigina 123
Norman, Jerry 102
Norman French 85
North American languages 119
North-east Caucasian family 96
North-west Caucasian family 41, 118
Norwegian 9
Nostratic idea 37–40, 43–4, 135n
noun classes 17–18, 21, 33, 54, 58n, 93
number systems in pronouns 117
Nusu 22

Oceanic languages 86–7
O'Grady, Geoffrey N. 36n
Ohala, John J. 64n
Okinawa language 60–1
Old English 19n
Old Irish 79n
Old Testament 81
Olmsted, D. L. 40
Onishi, Masayuki 61n
origin of language 63–6, 73–4, 143

Pacific Islands 85–7
Pama-Nyungan hypothesis 36n, 37, 91
Pāṇini 128
Papuan languages 10n, 87–8
Paraguay 106
Paumarí 110
Pawley, Andrew 86
Payne, David L. 94n
Pedersen, Holger 37
phonemic analysis 149–50
phonetic borrowing 19
phonological borrowing 19
Pirahã 82n, 84
Plato 81, 128

polygenesis 66
Polynesian subgroup 50n
Portuguese 8, 62n, 110, 114
prestige languages 9n, 22–5, 79–80, 104–14,
 145–8
primitive languages, lack of 65–6
pronoun systems 117
pronouns, bound 55–7, 93, 123–4
proto-languages 45–9, 97–102, 142–3
punctuation of equilibrium situation
 73–85, 103–4

Qiang 16
Quechua 34n

Rankin, Robert L. 34
Rawang 69n
reconstruction 30–1, 42–3, 149–52
Reichard, Gladys A. 64n
religions, aggressive 78–9, 112–15
Renfrew, Colin 48n
retroflexion 19
Romance languages 29, 46
Ross, Malcolm 86
Russia 36–9, 135n
Russian 12, 20n, 83, 147–8
Russian-American Company 12

Sanskrit 14, 41, 46, 50
Sapir, Edward 14, 19, 21–2, 25, 70
Schmidt, J. 17, 70
Semitic languages 21
serial verb constructions 21
Sherzer, Joel 16
Shevoroshkin, Vitaly 39
Shibatani, Masayoshi 31–2
shifters 64
Shona 79–80
Siebert, Frank T., Jr. 48, 98n
Siegel, Jeff 60n

similarity, accidental 15n
Singhalese 28, 61, 119
Sinitic (Chinese) 102
Sino-Tibetan 102
Slobin, Dan I. 75n
Smith-Stark, Thomas C. 16
Snyman, J. W. 118, 119
social attitude towards language 10
Socrates 82
Sommer, Gabriele 144
sound symbolism 64
South American languages 50, 84, 94,
 108, 119–20
 see also Amazonia as a linguistic area
Southworth, Franklin C. 46
Spanish 8, 62n, 106n, 125
split-S system 122n
splitting of languages 58–63
Stankiewicz, Edward 13
Sub-Saharan Africa, see African
 languages
subgrouping 49–53
Subrahmanian, K. 53
Sumerian 81
suppletions 22
Swadesh, Morris 10, 35, 40
Swahili 41, 83, 144
Sweden 148
Swedish 146, 147
switch-reference marking 21, 25
Switzerland 106
synonymy, multiple 72–3
syntactic functions, marking 121–7
Systemic grammar 123n

tabooing 19, 26, 73
Tai-Kadai language family 16, 42n
Taino 107
Taiwan 9n, 86
Taiwanese 9n

Index

Tanzania 83, 143–4
Tariana 24–5, 123, 126
Tasmania 76n
Tasmanian 35n
Teeter, Karl V. 36
tenses 118–19
Thomason, Sarah Grey 11–12
Threlkeld, L. E. 112
Tibeto-Burman family 14, 102, 119
Tindale, Norman B. 89
Tjiliwiri initiation style 12n
Tok Pisin 110
tones 16–19, 33
Torres Strait, western language 119
Trubetzkoy, N. S. 98n, 99n
Tucano 114
Tucanoan languages 24–5, 120, 125
Tungusic language family 32, 38
Tupari 108
Tupí language family 84, 88–9
Turkana 119
Turkic language family 32, 38
Turkish 41
typological comparison 31–2
typologists, armchair 136n

Ungarinjin 123
Uralic family 32, 38, 41, 48, 100–1
Urdu 25
Ussher, James 36n

Vamling, Karina 118, 122
Vaupés River basin 24–5, 114, 120
Vedas 81
Vietnamese 41
vocabulary, core 10–12, 20, 36–7
Vogt, Hans 11, 36

Warlpiri 13n, 57, 72
Weinreich, Uriel 22
Welmers, Beatrice F. 124
Welmers, William. E. 64n, 124
Western Desert language 26n, 72–3
Williamson, Kay 32, 33
Wilson, Robert 25
Woodlark Island 10
word order, see constituent order
words, phonological and grammatical 128
writing 80–2, 112
written records 29

Xerente 64n
!Xũ 118, 119

Yanyula 58n, 113
Yeeman tribe 107
Yimas 110
Yir-Yoront 64n

Zepeda, Ofelia 136
Zimbabwe 79–80